THE UNTOLD TRUTH

Beyond Belief

John Anderson

To Richard.
With thanks and appreciation for your sharing with me your
erudition, wide knowledge and deep understanding.

CONTENTS

PREFACE

War, it could be argued, is today's greatest threat to the world. Nuclear war can take place at the touch of a button. The other man-made threats to our fragile planet take longer to solve: global warming, over-population, pollution and so on.

Over the years, we have tried to use *reason* to solve the problem of war, but to no avail.Humanity's relative lack of moral and psychological progress, and its ignorance and inability to come across factual, basic, Truth, about itself, is no excuse. Until the Truth is come across, we will continue in the same chaotic, dangerous, way.

So, the most important basic question today, in order for us to be able to know where and how we can heal this disease, is What is Truth?

. . . .

This study began as a private, personal investigation. It is an attempt to answer the question: How can we come across Truth?

In making this enquiry into Truth—a venerable pursuit - I attempted to do this in as faithful a way as possible. This required an honest, open-minded attempt at meeting the challenge. This insertion - in the form of an 'apologia,' which is my excuse for deciding to share this work - is due to its surprising outcome; which is 'beyond the belief' that I had at the outset. So, rather than consign the study to the waste paper basket, I felt that I should share it. The approach taken in this study, requires nothing but a desire to discover Truth; without having to rely on anyone else's opinion. The only requirement is an open mind.

#

So, we are here seeking an answer to the question: What is Truth?

*Can we wake up and come across the Truth?

*It is light that makes everything visible.

#

The following three quotes below refer to my having used many people's writings to add to my own input; this done in order to address mankind's eternal interest in the deeper mysteries of life.

"When you take stuff from one writer it's plagiarism, but when you take from many writers it's called research."

'The love of Truth seeks holy leisure? The necessity of love undertakes righteous action.'

It could be said of me that in this study I have only made up a bunch of other men's flowers, providing of my own the string that ties them together.

#

Some quotes referring to Truth:

*The inquiry of truth, which is the love-making, or wooing of it; the knowledge of truth, which is the presence of it; and the belief of truth which is the enjoying of it; the sovereign good of human nature.

Francis Bacon (English 1625)

* And you shall know the truth and the truth shall make you free.

St. John 8:32

* The truth is to be lived; it is not to be merely pronounced by the mouth.

Hui Neng (Chinese, 638-713)

* Mankind has been concerned throughout the ages to discover or live in 'Truth'.

Krishnamurti : (Indian 1895-1986)

> > > > >

PART ONE - SETTING OUT!

1- INTRODUCTION

Despite **thousands of years of prayers for peace**, peace in which our children and their children would live in safety, seems to be as far away as ever.

As Thomas Hardy wrote after the First World War:

> 'Peace upon earth!' was said.
> We sing it,
> And pay a million priests to bring it.
> And after two thousand years of mass
> We've got as far as poison-gas.

> 'Christmas 1924' T. Hardy (1928)

And, showing the stupidity of war:

> Yes, quaint and curious war is!
> You shoot a fellow down
> You'd treat if met where any bar is
> Or help to half-a-crown.

> 'The Man he Killed' T. Hardy (1909)

Humanity behaves often with love and compassion, but we can also act with great cruelty. The primary source of our controllable behaviour is the great advantage that we have over other animals: our large brain.

\#

So, does thought have any part to play in this problem?

It is very interesting that, as *thought* is so important in our lives, we seem not to take a lot of thought about thought itself!

Obviously, humanity's condition today is due to our ability to think. We have such incredible mind power that we are able to act creatively, to change the *Natural Order* and produced ever more comfortable and easy living for many.

This advantage to *technological* progress is offset by our lack of progress *psychologically*: our own relationships. So it can be said that, while our technological progress has been very rapid and has been of great benefit, and will always be so in many ways to us, thought that has produced this success has in fact produced much suffering. Mankind has been unable to make corresponding progress psychologically in order to manage the changes in our everyday lives, causing unnecessary suffering to the human race itself and also throughout Nature.

> We need to know when thought is useful and where and when it causes harm. Also what role has thought to do in our search for Truth?

>>>

2 - LIFE'S MYSTERIES

If it is assumed correctly that one's wish in life is to be happy, it is necessary to understand the fundamental truths of life. Ignorance is no excuse—mistaken actions in life will lead inevitably to unhappiness.

Now, life throws up many questions, the answers to which mankind has sought for millennia. A basic question can be thought to be the mystery of existence itself. It produces questions such as: What is reality? and What is consciousness? As science works to find answers to these mysteries, the emergence of modern science went through a traumatic experience: the important discovery in the early 20c. of the development of Quantum Theory. Scientists now realise that the more that is discovered the more we don't know; every explanation creates new problems. A major failing of science has been the continued inability to understand life and consciousness. Meanwhile much work is being made on reaching solutions to these questions.

In the meantime, as life is short, this study will avoid discussing theories concerning these mysteries—whether scientific, philosophical or theological—except to refer to them briefly where it is helpful. The study's approach will be to look at mankind's mysteries through our own individual *experiences*; our own everyday eyes. In other words, referring to the two specific questions mentioned above, making use of our own experience of reality and consciousness. By doing so, the study sets out to shed light on the underlying causes of humanity's problems and to point to possible solutions.

#

Our knowledge comes from our experiencing life. This experience comes from two perspectives: internally and externally. In this chapter some of life's basic mysteries will be briefly considered.

One mystery is the mystery of our inner world: our *life within* which is our subjective experience.

The starting point in any exploration of the nature of what ultimately **is** must be the fact of self-consciousness. Who am **I**? Of one thing I am certain: I exist.
But is my body me? Is my brain me? Do *I have* this brain or *am I* this brain? I sense that this brain is an organ in my body and I assume I have some control over it. I cannot see or feel it? We know in the same way that we know any other organ in our body. We just feel that this is located behind the eyes, for instance. So, if *I* have this body, if it is mine, **I** must be something other than this body. I am intimately connected to it but different from it. Throughout life we all experience this unchanging primary fact of life.

Together with this primary experience we need to be open to questions about our other inner experiences, such as: Who or what is this *self* or 'I'? Is my ego, which seems so variable, my real self? What is my mind and where does it come from? How do *I*, the observer, perceive *me*, the observed? Can mentation (mental activity) alone enable me to come across Truth?

Alexander Pope put it this way:

Know then thyself, presume not God to scan;
the proper study of mankind is man.
Placed in this isthmus of a middle state,

A being darkly wise, and rudely great.
With too much knowledge for the sceptic side,
With too much weakness for the stoic's pride,
He hangs between; in doubt to act or rest,
In doubt to deem himself a God or Beast;
In doubt his mind or body to prefer;
Born but to die, and reas'ning but to err;
Alike in ignorance, his reason such,
Whether he thinks too little or too much;
Chaos of thought and passion, all confused;
Still by himself abused or disabused;
Created half to rise, and half to fall;
Great lord of all things, yet a prey to all;
Sole judge of truth, in endless error hurl'd;
The glory, jest, and riddle of the world!

Let's temporarily name this mystery an **enigma**.

#

Then there is the mystery of our outer world: our
life outside which is our *objective experience*

This mystery of life is a world of material
phenomena and sense perception.

Again, if we are open to question it: Do we have a direct
reliable knowledge of our outside-world; the world of nature,
and the social world that we share with our fellow men and
women? What exactly is nature—often named *creation*? We
depend on the experience of our senses, our perceptions, to
inform us of what we can know about our outside world.
However, is the world we think that we know the true
world? For instance, we experience the outside world as
one of colour and noise. But the mystery is how this can be,
since presumably, there would be no colour or noise in the
universe without the sensing of eyes and ears. It is these
which sense and transmit certain types of vibrations for the

brain to receive their impacts. These sensorial impacts that we perceive as colour occur through certain processes in the brain. We see things and take them to be *actual*. They are definitely *real* to us, for 'seeing is believing'. But is our seeming-reality *the* actuality: that which *actually* is? The only things we can know directly, in themselves, are those *conditions* that go on inside, in our heads.

This mystery we'll name, also temporarily, a **riddle.**

#

Thirdly, as it is experienced by too many throughout history to be ignored, we must consider the mystery which can be described as the 'Beyond.'

This is that which is experienced outside of, *beyond,* our *objective experience* and 'beyond' our inner surface-mind's subjective experience.

This is the mystery of the 'Beyond'—seemingly *beyond* both our inner and outer landscapes. This **mystery** has been given many names by those who throughout history have claimed it to *be*: both those who have claimed to have experience of it and by those who have given reasons and/ or explanations for it to be. It has led to the production of the many and varied religions and spiritual traditions that we have today. This mystery of the consciousness of a *beyond* has its source in what is the raw material of religion and also the inspiration of a great deal of the arts and philosophy. It is a consciousness of something unseen. It is that which is not seen in the external world of matter, but it is interwoven with it. This may be named a 'mystical' or 'spiritual' experience.

However, the 'Beyond' remains *philosophically* unprovable. This particular dimension of life is intangible. Because it is not open to the mind directly, because it is not manifest, it is often classified as a 'spiritual' dimension.

This study will be mainly concerned with the truth of this mystery.

#

Each of these three aspects of life is often considered isolated from the others. Often, we approach these mysteries of life in a piecemeal fashion: one at a time, as if they are separate unconnected departments of life.

If we do so—and it is not suggested that we should—then the order in which we tackle them **is** important.

#

First, we must start with the **enigma** which is 'me'.
Without knowing the answer to this mystery of my *inner* world, the conclusions we reach about the other two puzzles, the *outside* and the *beyond*, may be—very likely—faulty.

This is because the 'self-conscious me' uses the *me's* (my) own mind. Our mind can be compared to a basic computer hardware component, called the *Central Processing Unit* (CPU). If that should malfunction or be programmed incorrectly, the results it produces will very likely be unreliable—but, unfortunately, likely to be believed. So we must similarly look to see whether the cause of our troubles is emanating from *our* 'CPU'; which is, of course, our brain or mind. The human brain is such a marvelous organ and serves us so well we tend to believe it serves us well in every way. But it does have a product which contributes to many of our troubles; troubles which are so important that they may ultimately destroy us. We do not see that mentation, the thoughts and other mental processes of our minds, are the cause of many of the problems that we have. This is because they emanate from the same source from which we try to solve them: the mind's processes themselves. Thoughts have helped mankind enormously; so much so that we see no wrong having them. We think that we can solve our (thought-produced) problems by the use of thought alone.

#

> Truth can be thought of roughly as:
> honest and faithful to *That Which Is*.

The Latin word *verus* means 'that which is'. The mind therefore has to be straight, honest and faithful for truth to be. That means that there must be no clever, often subconscious, tricks of the mind to fool one into *thinking* that: '*This is the truth*'. This is often caused by self-deception or wishful thinking. A certain state of mind is necessary; it needs to be open, awake and alert for truth to be come across. Later, in Chapter 7, this all-important condition will be considered.

Truth is both a *perception* and an *action*. The action of truth clears the mind of '*That Which Is Not*' and brings one to some realisation of '*That Which Is*'. Truth is *about* 'What Is' but acts *in* 'What Is'. As will be considered later, in Chapter 8, the source of Truth is like the source of insight; it is beyond what thought can understand.

#

This **mystery** of the 'beyond' has never been proved or disproved: whether or not there is a THAT, or a THIS, which is given many names: *God, Being*, the *Beyond, Nature*, the *Universal*, the *Immeasurable*, the *Void, Father, Mother*—or whatever name that one wishes to give 'IT'.

In this controversy:
- Some will have no doubt that IT does exist and that therefore there is no mystery.
- Others equally reason that there is nothing more to this third dimension than material creation itself. These people think likewise that there is no mystery.

One needs an **open mind**; *which requires courage for a religious believer.*

*In his poem 'The Darkling Thrush', Thomas Hardy sums up a lot of
people's feelings concerning this third mystery of life.
He compares the doubts of the 'passionless man' with the joyous
outpourings from the thrush. The thrush, unlike the man, seemed
to be aware of something unseen, something joyous.*

I leant upon a coppice gate
When Frost was spectre-gray
And Winter's dregs made desolate
The weakening eye of day.
The tangled bine-stems scored the sky
Like strings of broken lyres,
And all mankind that haunted nigh
Had sought their household fires.

The land's sharp features seemed to be
The Century's corpse outleant,
His crypt the cloudy canopy,
The wind his death's lament.
The ancient pulse of germ and birth
Was shrunken hard and dry,
And every spirit upon earth
Seemed fervourless as I.

At once a voice arose among
The bleak twigs overhead,
In a full-hearted evensong of joy illimited;
An aged thrush, frail, gaunt, and small
In blast-beruffled plume,
Had chosen thus to fling his soul
Upon the growing gloom.

So little cause for carolings
Of such ecstatic sound

Was written on terrestrial things
Afar or nigh around
That I could think there trembled through
His happy good-night air
Some blessed Hope, whereof he knew
And I was unaware.

#

The **riddle** of life involves ALL aspects of our life; our inside, outside and, if there is such a thing, the 'beyond/spiritual' dimension.

However, in order to approach Truth, which is *all-encompassing*, life must be considered properly as a whole.

#

At the outset in order to *dis*cover or *un*cover the truth of the matter, sides must *not* be taken.

Whatever anyone's present opinion or viewpoint of this 'beyond', **which need not be changed**, there is this mystery:

Is there, or is there not, something not manifest beyond THAT/THIS which we all physically sense?

#

If the **mystery** of the 'beyond' is to have any chance of being realised at all, it must be by the individual—him or herself.

And at this beginning point in the study we have to say that: 'me'—my true self or soul or whatever name one wishes to use —is an **enigma**. It is not 'Who do you **think** *you* are?' but:

'Do you really **know** who *you* are?'

Chapter 5 will consider this matter.

Only from the inside of this **enigma** will the **mystery**, in which the **riddle** of life resides, be solved.

Borrowing a well-known expression:

Life may be thought a **riddle**, wrapped in a **mystery**, inside an **enigma**.

\#

But before investigating the enigma of who we really are, we need to set down the rules needed to conduct this study. These are important if we are to avoid the dangers of being led astray; especially by this enigma—that which we *think* we are.

These rules are discussed in the next chapter.

> > > > >

3 -THE APPROACH

To what does the word 'Truth' point in the title,
'The Untold Truth'?

It points to the Universal *factual* truth. This is not the same meaning as *conventional* truth, which is used in everyday life and which depends on the individual.

> But at the beginning of this study the only *a priori* assumption must be that Truth is 'That Which Is.'

The first difficulty in attempting to come across the Truth is: How to approach the problem?

As mentioned, all we know comes from experience—our inner and outer experience. The only things we can know directly, in themselves, are our own mental states. It is the examination or observation of our own mental states which can provide direct knowledge. From the beginning people always have attempted to provide explanations of their experiences as to what the nature of the Truth means to them. These have enormously wide and varying explanations due to the wide variety of these introspective experiences.

So two, of many, approaches have been chosen in this study to find the solution to this question: What is Truth? These two come from two polar opposite directions used to discover Truth: a direct approach through experiencing, and the other indirect approach, through mentation, thought. This will enable both contrary approaches to be compared and examined.

The approach which, in general, has been used in the West can be called 'positive'. Generally, the other approach - the direct approach originating from the East - we can name as 'negative'. Two examples of each follow.

THE POSITIVE APPROACH TO TRUTH

From a Jewish Scripture, *Psalm 119: 160*
    All your words are true; all your righteous laws are eternal.
From a Christian Scripture, *John 14:8*
        Jesus answered: I am the way and the truth and the life.

THE NEGATIVE APPROACH TO TRUTH

From the writings of J. Khrishnamurti (died 1986):
        Therefore, God or truth or what you will is a thing that comes into being from moment to moment, and it happens only in a state of freedom and spontaneity, not when the mind is disciplined according to a pattern.
From Seng-ts'an (died 606)
        The Great Way is not difficult for those who have no preferences. When love and hate are both absent everything becomes clear and undisguised. If you wish to see the truth then hold no opinions for or against anything.

                                #

Setting principles at the outset is essential.
  ·   The approach must not favour any one 'claim to the Truth' over another claim.
  ·   No method is to be formulated. From the beginning there are to be no axioms or other 'starting' factors—except that mentioned below this chapter's title..
  ·   Hence all opinions, prejudices, beliefs, assumptions and conclusions are to be avoided as far as possible.

                                #

The approach then is to consider the two polar opposite

approaches in parallel.

First, the traditional 'Western' religious view of Truth. This can be described as a *Positive Approach.* This uses a verbal *statement of belief.* This is termed *positive* because one can say: "The Truth is …so and so". Examples of this approach to Truth in this study have to be mainly from the Christian perspective as this is the tradition I know best. However, a similar exercise could use any other religion or philosophy. In so doing one should also be able to see where this particular religion or philosophy stands in relation to the following second type of Approach.

This second way of 'Approaching Truth' is called the *Negative Approach.*

This approach can indeed lead to positive outcomes and thus the word 'negative' should not bring with it the usual connotations. This uses the 'Seeing or experiencing of What is' as its *modus operandi.*

> By approaching from these two opposite directions a greater understanding of the 'truth' may be perceived.

An important rule to note throughout: there is no intention of making any criticism of any particular religious or non-religious belief, or opinion. Neither is there an intention of changing anyone's present beliefs or opinions.

However, the study may *challenge* what is believed or may result in a greater *understanding* of what is believed.

Basically, the question is: 'Am I really happy?' This is, surely, what we all would like to be.

#

The main test of this negative approach, unlike the positive, is that it is of *universal* appeal. No one should feel excluded, whatever their circumstances.

From the outset some may say: 'I am certain that my beliefs

are the Truth'. However, if one has this *certainty*, it is worth considering a statement made by Lord Winston[1] in which he expressed the view that:

'Science and religion should be about **un***certainty*. Being certain in these fields is dangerous.'

Faith and *courage* are needed. The meaning of 'Faith' here is: 'having the courage to face up to *facts* ... and then seeing where they take one.'

#

It is important to note the following CAUTION: that in this study we should be careful not to throw the baby out with the bath water! We are warned that, when there is a loss of faith, and the 'old order' is thrown over for whatever reason, there is much potential danger.

It was Jesus who warned us in a parable[2] that the perceived outcome of an idealistic cause may not be the one originally desired[3].

For instance, one could possibly feel after studying this approach that: 'belief' itself is a cause of major problems and should be rejected and therefore thrown out. When a strongly held belief—such as a religious belief that gives one reassurances of security—is doubted one's world can seem to be swept from under one's feet. This can lead to despondency and possible fear.

The **CAUTION** is that the belief need not be rejected. In this study, for instance, it will be seen that instances from Christian writings (and other faiths too could be used where they reflect the truth) that the words point towards that which the Negative Approach is also pointing. The study in this way can help and can indeed strengthen the belief where the writings *point toward* the truth. There can indeed be a synthesis between them which can be helpful. And so one can, by not rejecting the faith or belief, 'translate' some of the myths and stories into the truth to which they are referring.

Creeds, tenets and so on can possibly be adhered to if one has an understanding of *What Is*. No hypocrisy is involved here!

#

Having understood that - in seriously attempting to find a solution to the causes of humanity's 'inhumanity,' - it is necessary to *suspend* temporarily *all* beliefs. These are beliefs that are used in the Positive Approach as to what life's *riddle* is all about. As stated above, this could demand some courage from some. But it should be remembered that it need be only a temporary suspension for the duration of the study. The outcome may be that the belief remains unaltered, or it may remain but with a more strongly held view as being better understood with regards its relationship with Truth.

At the outset, as mentioned in the 'rules' for this study above, we cannot propose an *appropriate* method. A method has to come from a *predetermined* source. But as we are to have no preconceived outcome, we cannot have a method to achieve this unknown outcome.

The starting 'goal' is simply to discover, or come across, Truth; which at this point may be defined as: *That Which Is.'*

So keeping to the rules, if someone says: *'The truth is ...* so and so', why should he or she be believed or trusted? Why place trust in one belief any more than in any other— including trust in a preacher or a prophet, or any book however sacred; a teacher, a saint, or a guru; or politician, philosopher, psychologist, scientist—anyone else?

Could one's belief perhaps be due to the random chance of what one's parents believe?

So the only possibility of finding the truth, as stated above, can only be by *oneself*. That is, if it is at all possible to come across

Truth, it must be by the *individual*. So what is one's course of action if no one else's solution can be accepted? How do we know what to do?

#

Truth at this stage can be defined as: **That Which Is**. This definition can be agreed *universally*.
The definition does not state that Truth is '*That Which Was*' nor '*That Which Is to Come*'. It therefore refers only to the **present**. Truth, therefore can only be known in the present **now**. Truth simply **is.**

Truth already exists; for it **is**. The phrase '*coming across the Truth*' is used because we do not *find* it; for Truth is not lost. Truth is the fact; it is **now** in actuality: It is *That Which Is*.

What blinds us from seeing the Truth? We need more 'light' rather than more knowledge.

Jesus could have been referring to this when he said:
'For judgment I have come into this world, so the blind will see and those who see will turn out to be blind.'

The blind, here, are those who *admit they cannot see and* those who see are those who *claim to see*.[4]

#

Much of the second Approach is based on **pointing** to the truth.

The '*finger points to the moon'; it is the moon that is the subject.* Pointing is necessary; it usually consists of visual, verbal or symbolic myth or metaphor. The moon is the object. Once that is known, the finger can be forgotten. Some go no further than believing in the 'finger'. As it were, they suck the finger for comfort!

In this so called '**negative approach'** there is no map or plan. It is called a 'Way;' there is no planned route. One leaves the safety of the harbour without a chart, as there is no chart to be trusted at this point.

*Jesus did not generally teach any methods or practices aimed at helping us to discover the Truth about what he claimed was God, the Father. One of his commands was to believe in him. He said that to know the Truth we should **follow** him. He gave no directions for us to follow for ourselves. When Jesus said to his disciples that they knew where he was going, they replied that they didn't know. 'So how can we know the way?" they asked. Jesus answered: "I am the way and the truth ..."[5]. The command was to follow him wherever it led the disciple. He did not give a chart. He said that he would lead them: 'I am the Way'. What was asked of them was to believe or trust him. If they did that, he said, they would come face to face with Truth.[6]*

Those who start out on this 'Way-less Way' need to have courage. Should I believe a prophet who says: "I know the Truth"? Surely, there is no method for Truth's discovery; no formula, no plans, no patterns, no maps. This is because all directions will be through someone's *interpretation*.

#

The way a question is put is often very important to the outcome. So, if we ask 'How do we come across Truth?' we are expecting a method. A question like "*How* do we ....?" is put as a question with the possibility of an answer.

The way to begin this study is to assume that it *is an impossible question to answer*. By doing this there is no temptation to formulate a method, for one does not know how to proceed. One's mind goes blank! This is similar to asking 'How do I lift the milk jug?' You are not expecting a method as to *how*. You just lift your arm and do it —naturally. If it is possible for you to do it naturally, physically, you just do it.

The impossible question is this:

Can the mind itself come across the Truth?
It is impossible to answer because, in order to answer it, we would normally have to use the mind, itself. So firstly, we need to *understand* our minds, and hence the way our thought works.

#

Here we must be concerned with the use of thought; how do we use our intellect? Proper uses are, for instance, in order to map out a career or plan a holiday. This needs a positive *path*: the path being a method or a course of action which helps us travel from A to B. Thought deals with details of this kind for everyday life very successfully.
It is the part that thought plays in the *un-manifested* part of our lives that this study is mainly interested in because it is here where the basic problem lies. Here we are mainly concerned with the working of our minds; especially with our thinking: hence the main concern is with our *psychological inner life*.

#

If Truth is hidden, what hides it? What enables us to question our own wonderful existence? It is that we are *self-conscious* beings. The revealing of the Truth must be through our introspective experiences. Our Approach must therefore be *psychological*.

#

Analysis must not be used to see how the mind works in this approach. Analysis is very important in scientific researches, but it is of no use in this Approach. This Approach looks at the *resultant* workings of the mind.
It is the *outcomes* of our mind's psychological work that are important here.

It is not suitable that **That Which Is** is put under analysis, for Truth does not have parts. Truth cannot be divided up into fragments. Usually we see the *totality* of, say, a tree. The totality is made up of its parts, the fragments. A botanist can analyse it; studying its details. Truth has to stand as a complete Whole. The Whole gives meaning and significance to the details. Wherever one is, the view is always the same; the tree is the tree, from whatever angle it is perceived. The Approach also must stand as a *whole*, whatever one's present position is. The parts arrive and stay together; they are not brought together. The Whole of an organism, the tree, is greater than all the parts. All the parts of the tree, the trunk, the roots and the branches, make the totality of the tree. The significance, or meaning, of the tree is known when perceived as a whole. In a living organism, the parts *grow together*—or go together—with every part interrelating with and depending on every other part. The development of a baby is one miraculous example among an infinite number of examples from organic nature. The result of this is something more than the total—that is: the *whole* is more important than the *totality*. As with Life, Truth can be understood when we can perceive and have insight into the Whole[7].

Life in its Wholeness is in even the smallest part, even though its smallness may seem so insignificant. Life is greater than its parts.

Truth, if it is to be known, cannot be known by force; it must come of its own accord[8].

The window needs[9] to be open, figuratively, to have any possibility for a breeze to enter the room. A door needs to be opened for an entry to be possible.

#

In speculative philosophy we try to discover Truth without understanding the *Actual*—the Actual being: *That Which Is*. We should look at the actual facts in order to understand it and not waste energy in speculating about things which should or should not be. Speculative philosophy deals with concepts which are conceived in the mind and are kept in the memory. We are usually in the habit of trusting implicitly what thought is telling us. Thought, or the mind, can actually *cover over* an actual fact without our knowing it. This will be discussed later.

#

This negative approach to life is psychological. It is completely free from moralising—free of good and evil—and what one should or should not do. Each situation is unique. It recognises the friction caused by our being split between *what I am* (in fact) and *what I want me to be* (that is what my mind wants me to be). It is this that causes suffering. We need to start from where we are. Then the starting point will be with what actually *is*, not with what we think it ought to be.

#

It is a fact that as we are in ourselves so is the state of society. Society is a general reflection of its individuals. Thus we see the great importance of knowing ourselves. If we come to know this turmoil and confusion in ourselves—and which is reflected in society as a whole—we ask how can we bring order out of disorder?

By being aware of the danger of disorder then the problem is brought into the light. It is seen, not by analysis, but by *realisation* or *insight*. In truly seeing the problem and understanding the danger of disorder and the immense problems it causes, this *negative* fact brings order—which is a positive thing.

Notice that this positive order comes without positive force or method. The problem is not approached directly: that is, it is not approached *positively*. This is an example where a *negative* leads to an important *positive*.[10]

This must not just remain an intellectual theory. Through *realisation* can come an answer to the problem. This answer could produce a rejection of certain parts of our culture. With this denial there could come also a possible denial of the *self* which has created this kind of culture in the first place. Again this will be considered in more detail in a later section.

#

If all things are in *order* they are in their intrinsic[11], natural places. However we often try to create order unnaturally by setting up, in our minds, *systems*. These systems are such things as say, a religion, or a political dogma, a philosophical theory, an educational system to teach reading or, indeed, some kind of hypothesis such as answering the question: 'Who do you think you are?'

In the Approach used in this study there is no guidance as to the extent or the range of study; there is no *'frame to the picture.'* There is no frame or *system* in which to place any detail; but there is *order*. This is order in which things occupy their intrinsic, natural places.

Where there is disorder there is friction and therefore a waste of energy. Energy is needed to come across the truth. One could bring in the concept of *entropy* here (just as it can be applied to many areas of life). In this case we can say that there has to be low entropy in order to come across Truth.

A system is a framework, or a set of pigeon holes, into which we place details. These maintain the system and make it acceptable. This creates *order* in the mind. The mind is unhappy with chaos; it needs to understand and 'make sense' of things and concepts; the mind needs order. If one believed for instance that the sun rotates around the earth, until disabused of the error, it will remain a 'fact' for that person. It will be *real* to them; it will be their reality and life will be lived in the 'light' of that personal reality. In this orderly system there are various compartments. When anything new comes to the attention of someone's mind he or she tries to place it in a compartment of its ready-made system. Usually the order that we know will exist only within the framework of a system. For example, in a theological system of beliefs, all questions and problems are—often with great effort—fitted into the system until

it 'feels comfortable' to the believer[12]. However, if the new cannot be fitted into any of its existing systems it will try to regard it as irrelevant and the mind will try to ignore it. But if the new idea refuses to be ignored, the new will become an annoying disturbance to the mind until 'order is restored'.

#

Because this Approach to Truth has no (intellectual) framework it cannot be associated with any existing religious, scientific or philosophic system. The mind will therefore find it difficult at first to understand this *order* which has no *system* as there are no defined rules or methods of *'how to'*. These need to be made to fit into an organised 'framed' system. There may be an acknowledgement of a 'need'. But the need is not a method and is often a 'negative' thing (like the need mentioned above for a window or door to be open for the breeze to, *naturally*, enter). This Approach to life—*provided* we know how to look at this frameless picture—can be seen to be less complex than alternative approaches, such as using the intellect.

#

On the one hand my thinking mind itself creates an obstacle to the coming across of Truth. However, on the other hand my thinking mind is essential for the *pointing* to Truth. This very study, having to use words, is an example in it having to be so. We need to use words and concepts in order to point to things which *themselves* cannot be defined or described through words and concepts. This can obviously cause difficulty!

#

We cannot say directly what Truth is. If one says: "The Truth is ......," then that cannot be the Truth.

　　　For instance, it is not *true* to say: "I am now looking at a piece of paper". In order to be more accurate and factual, what should be said is: "*That*—that which I see in front of me—is *called* 'a piece of paper'". There is a difference between a piece of paper (the actual thing) and a "piece of paper" (the description). That is:

the description is not the described.

We do not need to define it like this in everyday life; we know what we mean by the word 'paper': for 'paper' is a tangible thing to describe.

However it points to a very important fact: our actual thoughts and language by which we communicate, however important at this level, can only *point* to the truth.

#

Truth is *not* static, it is *not* fixed, it has *no* path, it fits into *no* system, It *cannot* be analysed. Realising this from *negative* facts which one is aware of, Truth may come to be known as enormously positive: vital and living. So Love and Beauty are to be approached in the same way; for Love is *not* jealous, *not* greedy, *not* proud, *not* ambitious.   Love and Beauty have no opposites. This Love is not the love which has an opposite, hate. Also this Beauty is not the beauty which has ugliness as an opposite.

Paul explains Love with many negatives: 1Cor 13:4 - 7

#

The Approach seems anti-intuitive to our normal way of thinking of life and its problems. It is not just a change in the way our lives are led. We are not just changing one belief for another one. If it should be said: '*There must be no belief,*' then '*No belief*' becomes the new belief—it will *still* be a belief. It is a *totally different* dimension of living. It provides a fundamental change in our psychological condition.

#

But this can only be found out by the individual. This, with its difficulties, will be considered later. The way forward is simple and exciting.   So to understand the Approach better what is needed is some understanding of the workings and products of the mind.

This uses the fair assumption that the individual mind is *basically* similar to everyone else's mind; varying only in degree of capacity and experience. The mind is the subject in the next section.

>>>>>>>

4 – OUR HOMEMADE WORLD

One of the major reasons for the problems that humanity brings upon itself is that it is the way *thought* acts. We are generally unaware of the full effects of thought.

The problem can be illustrated by the way in which a book is read:

As your eyes skim across the marks on the page, you concentrate one hundred percent, quite rightly, on the meaning of the words. Rarely are you aware of what is *actually* being seen and felt as you turn the page. As you concentrate on the meaning of what is written you are not conscious of what in fact is happening. You are rarely conscious of such things as the abstract letter-symbols (in the form of conventionally agreed marks on the paper). You do not notice consciously each individual mark. You automatically interpret[13] the groups of symbols that your eye skims over; interpreting into understandable communication between the writer and you. (At least what you yourself *think* the writer intends to mean). You do not 'see' the spaces between the marks or the vehicle on which the marks are carried, which is the paper itself. Also you are not usually conscious while you read of the way the pages feel, how they are bound together and so on.

Now, of course, reading as we do in our normal way is correct and quite natural. The mind is functioning as it should.

Obviously if we were aware and observing these things as we read, we would not get far. So the brain is clever in this situation. But it does illustrate the fact that we are seldom consciously aware of our brain's activities—unaware of its conscious and un-conscious state. In our everyday thinking, we are totally engaged with the content of thought. We feel that we are awake; fully awake to everything. However in this study it is needful to be aware of the results of thought's operations. In this way we may expose it to the light of its consequences in our lives.

It is important to realise, for instance, that the brain is at the centre of *all* our activities. (It was called the CPU, the Central Processing Unit, earlier.) If this is not understood, anything done will possibly have no meaning or cause problems. Do you know for instance why you have suddenly thought of something; or what causes you to remember, or desire something? Do you know what your next thought will be?

So, while the mind itself is wonderful and valuable when functioning as it should, it is essential to know where it can cause problems.

#

Some of the problems caused by the activities of the mind, thought being one of them, are now discussed.

Thought leads to **fragmentation**.

Our minds cut the world up into neat parts in order to understand it. Otherwise it would be hard to analyse and deal with it.
Examples are:

> Dividing the world into lines of latitude and longitude;
> Dividing ourselves into nations; calling ourselves, say,
British, others American, French and so on.

So that we can understand the world, live in it more comfortably and dominate it, we have used thought to divide the world and life into convenient bits.

In actuality *the universe is a whole and we are one with it.* The life of the Universe and our lives are interdependent.

#

Our culture and education bring us up and prepare us to compare ourselves with each other. *Comparison*, an activity of the mind, is a cause of fragmentation.

This comparative activity of the mind creates the struggle to become something we are not and get something we do not have. At the level of the personal self, personal self-ambition and self-competition are good and beneficial to a certain extent. However outwardly in society, comparison in our relationships with others bring about a type of progress that leads to conflict; which can lead to suffering—usually of the innocent. A child's education, rather than being competitive with others as it is, should be without comparison.

As an example, sport has been elevated in our society to an ever more extreme degree of seriousness—leading to elation (for the one winner) and depression (for everyone else), to cheating (using drug enhancing super-human performances) and corruption in local and international competitions.

#

The 'surface' differences, or *form,* of peoples across the whole of humanity, are comparatively small. Our 'outsides' differences, in other words, are comparatively only skin-deep. This is true also concerning our 'inside' differences. All humanity has inherited brains and minds, and physical and emotional needs, which differ only by degree of functioning. So, each individual human being can claim that:

'I am in all respects the same, basically, as any other member of humanity'

This sense of people being different in reality to oneself is enhanced when peoples go to war with each other. We see how easily an enemy becomes a friend and vice versa. Recent examples are only too obvious to need pointing out. During the 'enemy stage' events, however horrific, can be justified against the foe: "They are less than human." All this is forgotten, if not forgiven, when the foe becomes the friend. Often my enemy's enemy becomes my friend. In all this mind-produced 'mad' behaviour, we do not realise[14] that fundamentally we are the same.

#

Consider little newborn babies. Like stem cells they are all alike, except for superficial features such as skin colour. They are all the same little human beings whether they are born in Egypt, in China, in Israel, or in Ireland.

This sameness disappears immediately the baby is born. The child becomes (through the workings of thought) an Egyptian child, a Chinese boy or girl, an Israeli infant, or an Irish baby. Identification with its place of birth or parents' nationality becomes predominant. All this is the result of thought. Now this is benign and acceptable if one sees that a baby is born into a society in which it will be taught its language, history and so on. But this thought-identification with a particular group separates the child from other groups.

#

When we use the mind's image and the imagination of separation then we perceive things and people as separate. We make them separate, drawing a line between, for instance, countries and religions—these being often inextricably entwined.

One could say that our bodies are individual but there are close connections on levels of communication. A language can only exist because of a collective culture and a society. Thought determines what is connected and what is not.

Albert Einstein said:

> *Nationalism is an infantile sickness. It is the measles of the human race.*

Nationalism is not the only major cause of fragmentation of the human race produced by mind-made reality. Another partner in the cause of divisiveness is *religion*. Indeed, there is often a close relationship between religion and nationality.

Probably religion eclipses nationality as being even more dangerous. As with national identification, religious identification can be a benign influence and it can be for good if children are taught to ultimately decide for themselves what to believe on maturity. This is not so applicable to nationality of course.

The result of religion in the very early years of a child is the identification of the child with its parents' religion. The child has no choice in this most important matter. When this happens, the baby leaves its 'human' context and becomes a Moslem child, a Christian child, a Jewish child and so on. To speak of children, who are very many years away from choosing for themselves, as being a 'Moslem child', a 'Christian child', a 'Hindu' or a 'Jewish' child is a good illustration of how thought acts dangerously. The existence of 'Faith' schools, funded by the State, is an example of incoherent thinking, as it promotes, secularly, religious identification.

#

The following three quotes illustrate clearly the fragmentation of humanity which results from these mind-produced divisions.

The followers of the three (so called) 'Religions of the Book'—Christianity, Islam and Judaism—will each believe *one* of the following three very random extracts from their scriptures as being true, and the other *two* as false:

- At the name of Jesus every knee shall bow (New Testament)
- Mohammed is the Messenger of God, and those who are with him are hard against unbelievers, merciful one to another. (Koran)
- Blessed are you, O Lord our God, King of the universe, who made distinction between the holy and the profane, between light and darkness, between Israel and the nations. (The Siddur, Jewish Prayer book)[15]

With reference to this, Paul wrote that in God's eyes there was no difference between peoples of different **races**, **genders** and **social class,** when he wrote:

"There is neither Jew nor Greek, slave or free, male nor female".[16]

#

*W*e can say that actually we are all members of one race —the human race. We have the same basic material *brain* and are the same *physically*. Differences are relatively minor and skin-deep[17]. However, despite this, we are fragmented from each other as a result of our minds' activities. All, without exception, celebrate their groupings (nations, tribes) through symbolism: flags, stirring anthems and so on, so we differentiate ourselves from everyone else—us and them. All nations have pride in these things including the nation's memory. There can be no problem in this, providing one is aware of the problems of relationship it can produce.

The following is a brief extract from an article in the Radio Times (August 2013). It accompanied a series: *The Story of the Jews.* It was written and narrated by the historian Simon Schama, who is himself a Jew. He wrote:

> '*For the Jews, remembering is who they are, it is a religious obligation ... So, to be Jewish is to be unthinkingly part of an immense family of memory ...*'

(The two emphasised *is*'s are made in the original article.)

The article was accompanied by a photograph of a group of young boys waving Israeli flags.

Again, Shakespeare in his play *Merchant of Venice* illustrates the point of fragmented humanity (in this case between a Jew and a Christian) when Shylock says:

> *I am a Jew. Hath not a Jew eyes? Hath not a Jew hands, organs, dimensions, senses, affections, passions? Fed with the same food, hurt with the same weapons, subject to the same diseases, healed by the same means, warmed and cooled by the same winter and summer as a Christian is? If you prick us do we not bleed? If you tickle us do we not laugh? If you poison us do we not die? And if you wrong us shall we not revenge?*

The Merchant of Venice III, i v49-61

\#

A further mind produced problem is the production of **ideas**.

Some ideas produced by the mind can be a great danger also.

Concerning ideas, the following extract comes from the end of the series *The First World War* (Channel 4, November 2003). Summing the results of The First World War the commentator said:

'The **ideas** for which men fought have proved lasting: **democracy**, **religious faith** and **nationalism**.'

This shows that little was learnt when it was thought that this was the "war to end all wars." For it is these very three mind-made ideas—democracy, religious faith and nationalism —which divided people then—and they still do so.

Despite sending millions to destruction and misery the commentator said that these were "worth fighting for"! It is **nationalism** and **religious faith** that have been behind wars throughout much of history. And it continues of course to this day.[18]

'Fundamentalism' is a word that is complicated by the fact that there are many kinds of fundamentalists, not only in all three 'religions of the Book'—Christian, Jew and Moslem—but in every creed and in every nation.

And what does 'democracy' mean in practice? (How is it practiced? Is it free and fair? Even if so, we see results have been overturned by the more powerful 'outsiders' who did not like the outcome.) The very concepts of *democracy*, *religious faith* and *nationalism* themselves are open to wide interpretation and application. It can be seen that it is these three *ideas*—these three *products of the mind*—which are at the core of many wars and factions.

It is our *fear* which causes us to fragment into groups, so that we can ostensibly defend ourselves. But our need to defend ourselves is because we have divided into groups![19]

#

Another mind-produced problem is its ability to **Name,** or to *verbalise.* This is a thought process enabling us to differentiate between 'this' and 'that'.   As part of language, naming has enabled humanity to communicate. The value of thought is that we can create and manipulate our environment using thought processes.   We are very good at using thought for achieving these material aims. These processes are a feature of the mind. So where is the problem?

It is in the fact that thought can, *psychologically*, break up into parts something which in itself is complete—the whole includes all the parts.   Usually this actual 'background'— *the United Whole of Nature* in which these named things are embedded though actually existing—is 'invisible' to us.

It is important to know what actually happens when we see something.

Conventionally we assume that we see the rose; the eye and the seeing seem to be the same thing and it is 'me' doing the seeing. But the visual impact on the sensing organ and thence on the brain is, seemingly, immediately overcome by the mind's psychological response. This response is from the dead past.

The process of seeing needs three processes:
    1. **Sensing**. In this process the light-reflected shapes and colours are sensed by the eyes. These impacts on the appropriate organ of sense, the eyes in this case, have in themselves no meaning. Nor do the eyes give information. They give the *data- vision* of the outside world at any given moment.   The brain receives the impacts that the senses receive. The brain receives the sensorial impacts delivered from the sensing organs via an amazing network of nerves and by the use of a mysterious code language. The brain, with its factual memory, has a mechanism for interpreting these messages—at an incredible speed. The reflex mechanism of the brain works at a biological level for the

safety of the whole organism.   These impacts feed into the brain's memory.

2. **Selecting**. A single part of the visual field is selected; not only by that which the physical eye senses but also on a psychological basis—what the most interesting or relevant part of the visually field is sensed. The *brain* stores these facts as fed to it by the senses using its *factual* memory. However, the *mind* has a memory store of its own—a *psychological* memory. It is responsible for interpreting the sense impacts which reach the brain. [20]

3. **Perceiving**. The above sensed and selected field is interpreted—through past experience and memory—to result in something that we see. Usually our mind immediately reacts to the facts perceived. It does so by using thought— by verbalising, by naming generated from the psychological memory store. This store contains all our psychological past memories and its immediate reaction to the experience depends on the experiencer, the enjoyer, the hater, the chooser; in other words the **ego**. Due to this mind response to the sensed impact there is an immediate cut off, prematurely, to what facts the brain is receiving.

Words are taken to be our measure of reality. What is happening is that the seeing of the rose becomes a reality *because of* the eye. But actually, the eye and the seeing are two separate things. It is actually *the mind* that does the seeing. Unless the sensed impact is great enough, the psychological effect usually is greater than the factual impact received by the senses.

In this seeing, therefore, there are three components. There is, firstly, the rose—the material *object*—and, secondly, the eye that senses the light waves reflected from the rose. Both of these, the eye and the rose, are physically tangible material. Neither can *know* the object—the rose. The third component in this seeing is the *mind*. It is this mind, the mentality, that can *know* what the rose looks like. It is *the mind* which is the *knower* of the object's image.

The production of this pair of separate elements is known as **seeing**.

We see wonderful diversity in nature. In everyday life all that we perceive actually becomes our mind-produced *reality*. This mind-produced reality is *my* reality. My mind takes over completely all that is 'me' (inside), and all that is outside of 'me'. Normally this may or may not be close to the *actual, which* is close to *What Is*.

#

If a baby sees a 'rose' it will see a squiggly, colourful thing. An adult will say: "That's a lovely *rose!*" The name 'rose' *represents* the actuality of the thing, itself. The rose *itself* is the actual, that *which is*. If carelessly clutched its prickly stem will quickly remind one of its actuality! Any sound of course would have been adequate to represent the thing we name 'rose'; as of course it has in other languages: *rosa* in Spanish.

Shakespeare wrote: "What's in a name? That which we call a rose by any other name will smell as sweet"[21]

By *immediately* naming, we place an image that we have of a rose, for example, over our perception of it. This image divorces us from the reality of the thing itself. So the fact of the thing sensed by the eye, which is our **per**ception of it, is modified into a **con**ception. Our mind's memory, that is our *psychological* memory, identifies the thing perceived by our senses and names, or verbalises, the experience. To do so we must have had an experience of it before. It therefore is nothing new; it is from the past. The resulting perception is usually distorted by memory: our past experiences, prejudices and so on. Thus the rose itself in its uniqueness is seldom experienced directly. So how much more is this image-making exaggerated when in relationship to another *person*, rather than with a simple thing of nature? The factual world sensed is made into a 'homemade' reality in our mind.

#

We need to be aware of the usefulness of thought but also its limitations and, indeed, its potential for harm.   This realisation produces the fact that our 'normal' viewpoint is dangerously restricted.   Above all it hides the fact that our view should not be from a *symbolic reality* only. This view is produced by the mind when it comes within the area of activity of the self. It is when the mind is in this area of the 'self' that the mind's activity causes trouble. This 'self' or 'I' uses symbolic language which causes us to see only from a point whose centre is the '**I**'.

This 'I' is the central producer of the thinker and namer, the controller.

#

The mind produces a home-made reality. To escape from this restriction—the only way to obtain a view that is not restricted by this home-made reality of the mind—comes from within the *freedom of space* and *silence of the mind*[22].

#

So successful are words that we usually forget that: 'word-thought activity' only *represents* actuality.

Thought is abstract from *what is*. So thoughts with their words cannot actually bring us to the Truth directly. Thought is based on the past. An object seen is normally named—it seems that it is named *immediately*—if it is recognised. In order for this to happen, there must have been a former experience of the object and a learning and remembering of the name. Thought is based on time; time that is *chronological* time[23].

Truth, which is being described as That Which **Is**, can only be discovered in the present moment.

#

When a name is given to a tree, for instance, immediately it 'changes' in one's mind from when it is first seen. It changes from an *actual* colourful, complex object—which is THAT observed *part* of the Whole—into a "tree" which exists in our mind as memory. The word "tree" or "oak" becomes the observer's reality. The experiencing of the actual tree is covered over by the memory-image from the past which exists in the mind. It is this image which becomes a *reality* to the person who names it. In doing this there is no direct experience of **that** thing, which is now called "oak". Instead of a direct experience there is created a *distance* between the observer and the observed: the actual tree itself. Thus there is a duality: an observer and the observed.

Words are often given too much importance; often they are given an even greater status than that to which they refer!

#

The extract below refers to the abstract—and so possibly dangerous—nature of 'words'. It is from Shakespeare's Henry IV Part I.
In this case the word in question is '**honour**'. Falstaff is in philosophical mood and is challenging the concept of the word 'honour'. It is generally accepted that the concept of honour, especially related to the field of conflict, is a most valuable quality of character and that it is worth a great deal for a person to be considered as an honourable person. Falstaff sees that in trying to 'do the honourable thing' it can lead one into doing ill-advised things in order for it to be achieved. He concludes that, despite it being taken by society as an important notion of character, it could be foolish and may well be costly. The passage follows:

The Prince says to Falstaff: *Why, you owe God a death.*

Here Shakespeare uses the expression of, 'owing God a death,' to mean: that as God has lent us life through our birth, so we owe it to him to repay with our death.

The Prince then exits leaving the self-concerned Falstaff —a portly and comic figure who is no fighter, though he pretended to be in front of the Prince—to his thoughts. These are given in the form of a catechism—a form of question and answer:

Falstaff
Death is not due yet: I would loath to pay Death before his day. Why need I be so forward with him that calls not on me?
Well, 'tis no matter; honour pricks me on (as with a spur). Yea, but how if honour causes me to be killed when I come on? How then?
Can honour set a leg? No.
Or an arm? No.
Or take away the grief of a wound? No.
Honour hath no skill in surgery then? No.

What is honour? A word!
    What is that word honour? Air.
    (Ironically) A pretty statement of accounts!
    Who hath it? He that died o'Wednesday.
    Doth he feel it? No.
    Doth he hear it? No.
    It is insensible then? Yea, to the dead.
    But will it not live with the living? No.
Why? Detraction will not suffer it. Therefore, I will none of it:
    Honour is a mere coat of arms carried at a funeral;
    And so ends my confession of faith.
Falstaff exits.

Falstaff, having been accused of acting timidly, realises that the word 'honour' is just that: a *word*—but having psychological power which could seduce him into carrying out some physically perilous action. "Pricking his conscience"—as words can—and "Causing his death." The power of words, such as 'honour,' can force a person to carry out brave, but hazardous—possibly unhelpful—actions.

#

Language is often used by politicians, among others, to manipulate us into believing what they want us to believe.

An example[24] is the word *evil*, used instead of the more discussible word *wicked.* There can be no discussion about an evil person, country or empire. They are 'Devilish' to the core; whereas a 'wicked' person has a chance of being converted—or so it seems.

Another tragic example came in 2022, when Russia attacked Ukraine. The politicians named their action a 'Special Military Operation' - instead of the usual word 'invasion.' Did they think that, by this manipulation of language, it would make the resulting immense suffering caused, more palatable to the Russian nation?

#

Thought **is of the** *past.*

A Nobel Prize winning psychologist has written to say that memory plays a surprisingly larger part in our lives than one may be aware of. The 'remembering self' creates our reality more than our 'present-experiencing self'.[25]

'Thinking'—say, a new idea or an *inside* imagination—happens in the present. But 'thought' comes from past thinking. This past thinking does not just evaporate on having just taken place; it leaves a memory trace which becomes thought. Thought then acts automatically—so automatic, in fact, that one cannot forecast what one's next thought will be!

Thought can reinforce and maintain an emotion. Thought is a response from memory, from the past, from what has been done. Thus, we have thinking and memory. We also have 'feelings', suggesting an active present, being directly in contact with reality. There are also past-feelings which have been recorded and 'crop-up' or 'pop-up' into consciousness.

Altogether there is a false division between thoughts and feelings and between present-feelings and past-feelings. Indeed, the whole state of the body is affected by these. Just the way you think can get the adrenaline flowing.

The past and the future—that is the *psychological* past and future measured by the mind—are created by thoughts. An outcome of the wonderful gift of human consciousness is that it allows us, for instance, to be aware of our own future demise. However time, as measured by the clock, named *chronological* time, measures the past. The chronological past has occurred, but no longer exists. The chronological future will occur but it also does not exist at this moment. Hence it is only at this moment, sandwiched between two non-existing times, which is the only true time. But, *psychologically*, neither the past and the future times exist. They are not actual. These exist only within the mind in the form of thoughts.

#

Thoughts **separate the self** from the world. We experience 'My boundary is my skin: inside is 'me' and outside of this skin is the world'. But this experience can vary; for instance a rider may feel at one with her horse, or a zealot at one with his group. All this is imaged in the mind as thought. It can change with the situation; the image may vary between being more correct in some situations than other.

#

Thought is **participatory**.

Thought gives the impression that it is just telling you the way things are. However thought, itself, is **affecting** 'the way things are'.

The whole of nature is affected by thought; for example, the destruction of the ozone layer has come about, unwittingly, by thought.

Until thought is understood and *perceived* that it is actually controlling us, while at the same time giving us the impression that it is serving us and just doing what we want, we will never avoid the pitfalls of thought. The failing is that we are not aware that thought, although making out that it is merely *reporting* **what is**, is actually *influencing* **what is**.

#

Thought **makes a system**[26].

This system includes not only thoughts themselves but also things, past-feelings, present feelings, including the state of the body and even extending to the whole of society. Thought is a network which connects people in a process by which thought has progressed since it first evolved.

Every culture has myths or collective fantasies. Many of these enter perception as if they were actual realities.

"THAT" is the fact: that we do not see the fact actually.

There is a higher order of fact: we are not seeing the direct fact. We must start from the fact of **'That Which Is'**.

#

The whole system is faulty. This **systemic fault** affects the whole system in every part. Culture is held together by the system of thought.

This system has a flaw both collectively and individually. Suppose you say: 'I understand the problem so I will think about its solution.' But 'your' thought, that you are thinking about it, *is* part of the system itself. This thought that you are thinking suffers from the same fault—the *problem*—that you wish to solve! This underlies all the problems of the world.

#

Thought affects perception.

Thought is able to make you insensitive to all the reflexes[27] which might make you, for instance sleepy, or lively, or inattentive or forgetful and so on. Thought can take over control of those reflexes and manage them.

Thought can make you feel tired or very excited. It can make your mind skip from one point to another: notice how social conversations move slowly or suddenly from one topic to another.

#

This abstract world of thoughts and symbols is the 'home-made' world of the mind, because it is created by our mind and exists only in the mind.   We tend to dwell mostly in this abstract world bewitched by the word.

We can imagine the almost magical quality that the first humans must have felt for the word, or sound, which stood for themselves: their name.   That name became, for them, that very person.   To a seemingly magical extent the person's name became more important than the physical person, him or herself! The 'name' of a person *seems* to **be** that person. These two quotes illustrate the need and power of a name:

'Wrestling, I will not let you go, till I your name, your nature, know.' (Charles Wesley)[28]

'It is as wholly wrong to blame Marx for what was done in his name, as it is to blame Jesus for what was done in his.' (Tony Benn)

#

Some other examples where the word nearly becomes more real than the thing it stands for:

The spoken word *chocolate* or reading a *menu,* which cannot be eaten, can nevertheless cause salivation if one is hungry! Money is symbolic and will do us no good unless we can use it to buy, say, food. Bread, itself, is the actuality, not the word 'bread'. Also, the actual value of money depends on what people will give it. Wealth can be symbolised by associating it with bars of gold or figures on paper. But the actuality is that it only exists in our heads as an abstraction.[29]

Because these three things are tangible and well known to us we know we can use the words which point to them knowing that they will be understood. It should be kept in mind also that even in the fields of science, mathematics, literature and much of our thinking, as in other spheres in the *life-of-the-mind*, our minds divorce us from actuality: the Truth.

#

One of the problems created by the *life-of-the-mind* is that it divorces us from Nature. Many now live in a totally man-made and virtual environment; exacerbated by the rapid development of Information Technology. We are unable to cope psychologically with the rapid change of technology. Many seem to be unable to control the domination of this technology in our lives. The enormous amount of information we now have at our fingertips, both domestic and foreign, attracts our minds to spend much time in learning mostly about superficial things and worrying trends for the future. All this divorces us from nature and only strengthens our *home-made* world. Without the association with nature, in which actuality resides with its space and beauty, and amongst which we intimately lived until relatively recently, we will circle further and further into, quite literally, mad behaviour.

#

Percepts[30] become *concepts* by the thought process. Thoughts produce concepts, ideas and hence ideals. All these create the thinker's *reality*. A sensation is received, say the sight of an oak tree, and that actual perception is changed into reality for the receiver of the sense by thought. So *actuality* (THAT) becomes *reality* ('oak'). This is because there is a (psychological) space between the mind which senses it and the tree. In this is formed a duality: an observer and an observed. In this 'space' an interval of time occurs and in this interval thought takes place.

#

We go through life experiencing sensations, thoughts, feelings, desires, much of which is symbolised by words. We take this marvellous physical body for granted; giving it hardly a passing thought. We use it thoughtlessly; often to the extent of abusing the systems involved, such as making physical demands on it that are beyond its natural ability. We are usually more concerned, practically continuously, with the stream of endless thoughts that rampage through our minds.   This is what Huxley meant by saying that we live in our **'home-made'** world; living 'at home' in a world of conventional symbols.

#

We rarely experience naturally living in the 'given' world—the world as it actually is. This *living in the actual world* implies living in the Now, in the Present.   This living cannot be described in words. The description cannot be the described. The described will be from the past, however close that is. Every thought is of the past.

#

So our thoughts then take us from the *fact of the feeling*, and into a more fictional—homemade—world that our minds create.   It can be seen that the intervention of the mind's thoughts produce a world which is not necessarily the 'true' world.

#

We live in our own 'home-made' world by naming. Naming divorces us from Life. We are separated from it by trying to fix or grasp it—for we do not like change, we like certainty. But life, if it is actual life, always moves on inexorably like a fast-flowing river. A river is never the same from one moment to the next. The river, considered from a distance with its banks, has a longer lasting recognisable shape compared to the water in the river. The water of the river is the real river. However, from one moment to another, not one drop of water is the same at any point. Trying to live in an unchanging, secure world by naming and thought will only provide a series of past, unfinished experiences. It will not be life as *it is*. Life in this mode is like trying to catch a river in a bucket; it will only provide a bucket of water and not a river. A river must be *flowing* in order for it to be a river.

#

Experiencing is made up of individual cognitive 'now-moments'. Each of these 'mind-moments' dies and disappears completely for ever before the next one arises. There is **nothing** that is carried on from one *mind*-moment to the next. What can be left is a trace of the experiencing in the brain's memory.

#

We are dealing with our problems piecemeal. We are looking at symptoms; trying to solve one problem after another problem. We may be able to use a sticking plaster at times. But until we realise that there is something deeper that is generating these problems they will not be resolved.

What is the source of this trouble? How is it that we do not see that the process which causes these problems is the very same with which we try to solve them? [31]

It is the automatic mind-generated *thoughts* which cause these problems and it is the very same 'tool'—our mind/thought—with which we try to solve them. As seen in this chapter, thoughts create difficulties such as the formation of religions and nationalities. However hard throughout history we have tried to find a solution to these problems of living together in harmony, we have failed—disastrously! So thoughts are not the means by which satisfactory solutions can be found to our relationships; relationships which are of a psychological nature. We are proud of the achievements of thought—in the physical world the speed of technological progress has been phenomenal —but when thoughts act in any kind of psychological relationship they can become sources of troubles.

This would point to the fact that thoughts alone will not enable us come to Truth.

#

The mind's attempt to grasp the actual world through the use of thought will never meet with any long-term success.

Change is inevitable, however much we desire that life remain as it is. That is what we desire heaven to be like. But it is not the actuality on earth. And it is not what 'true' religion says must be.

As an example, among many, Jesus said:

'A seed must fall into the ground and die. If it does not it remains by itself. But if it does die it will produce much fruit.'[32]

The fact that **life is transitory** is summed up in the words of Shakespeare, when he says:

'All the world's a stage, and all the men and women are merely players ....'[33]   and

'Our revels now are ended. These our actors, Are melted into air, into thin air: And the baseless fabric of this vision, The cloud-capp'd towers, the gorgeous palaces, The solemn temples, the great globe itself, Yea, all which it inherit, shall dissolve, And, like this insubstantial pageant faded, Leave not a rack behind.'[34]

#

A river cannot be caught in a bucket. The bucket represents words and concepts which are formed in the mind, and the flowing water represents the experiencing which can never be caught, or put into words. Experiencing happens Now.

Experienc*ing* (something that happens in the present) becomes experience (something that happened in the past). This becomes thought and memory.

#

We cannot *think:* 'That Which Is' into actuality. What is thought or named or described no longer exists, for thought is ever only from the past.

These things have no existence, other than existing in the mind's memory. They are of course very useful, but we should be aware that it is divorced from the experiencing itself.

Therefore, when one says: 'God', in a prayer, or writes the word 'God,' or mentions 'God' in a sermon, it is a pointing toward **That** or **That Which Is**, which cannot be described or measured. If we want to know 'God,' if such an experience is possible, we will only be able to experience Him/Her/It in the present moment—or in the 'Presence'. This experience can only happen therefore in 'real' time; that is in the present moment only.

#

What is important is what lies *behind* any word or image—the actuality to which it points.

This could be a word such as 'God,' or the symbolism behind a painting, such as a picture, say of Jesus knocking at a door. It is the actuality that is of importance and not so much the analogy with which it is associated.

An image of the man Jesus, say knocking at the door ("Behold I knock at the door" of your heart) is not as important to a Christian as the actuality of the presence of Christ Jesus **now**. That is: the actuality, the knowing, that the Holy Spirit is wanting to enter that person's life now rather than just having the belief that it to be so.

"Here I am! I stand at the door and knock. If anyone hears my voice and opens the door, I will come into him and eat with him and him with me."

Rev 3: 20

#

Jesus said:
  'Before Abraham was born, I AM'[35]

Jesus speaks of the present moment. He did not say: 'I was' or 'I will be.'

But what other truths lie behind these words? To try to explain all that Jesus meant by this statement, would only lead to having to explain each explanation, one after the other, and so on forever.

Each one of us needs to know who their true 'self' is; asking the question: "Who am I?" Each one of us can only come to the truth by asking ourselves this question, no one else can do this for us.

It is reported that Jesus asked his followers who they thought he was[36]. The speculation or given answers to this kind of question is not in the remit of this study, as mentioned from the start. This kind of question is dealt with by theologians[37]. What one can do, in a study such as this, is to look at the facts that we have. Then ask the question: What is the relationship between some[38] of the reported statements and actions of Jesus, (or any other 'teacher') compared with the main— negative—approach to Truth being pursued in this study?

#

So, we see that most of the time we live—psychologically—not in the actual world but in the make-believe world of our minds, which we take to be our real world. It is as if the mind has caused a veil to be hung over our consciousness while we live, heedless that we are living in a virtual day-dream.

Paul used the illustration of a veil[39]; the veil which Moses put over his face to hide God's glory from the Israelites. He says they still have the veil today, since only in Christ (he claims) can it be set aside:

> 'for to this very day whenever Moses is read, a veil lies over their minds; but when one turns to the Lord (becomes open to his message), the veil is removed. Now the Lord is the Spirit, and where the Spirit of the Lord is, there is freedom. And all of us, with unveiled faces, seeing the glory of the Lord as though reflected in a mirror, are being transformed into the same image from one degree of glory to another, for this comes from the Lord, the Spirit.'   *2 Corinthians 3.12-4.2*

The question follows: if we seem to live in a home-made world of the mind, what is this other, *given,* world and is it accessible? And if it is, how can we enter it?

But, before we can attempt to answer these questions, it is important to tackle the *enigma* of who we really are.

As mentioned in Chapter 2, if we misunderstand this central problem we may come to an incorrect result. Having in mind the dangers that are produced by the mind, by our thoughts, it is prudent to look at the potentially most dangerous product that thought has created.

> > > > >

5 - KNOWING YOUR SELF

In other living creatures ignorance of self is nature;
in humans it is vice"

Boethius

It seems that without the knowledge of who we actually are, we will go on acting in the same old way. We need to confront the enigma of our own identity.

We are blessed as a species in having a 'Central Processing Unit', our brain.[40] This is where operations are controlled and executed. It has evolved over time to become, as far as we know, the most remarkable organ in the universe.

\#

Some features of the brain/mind are worth considering briefly to aid in the coming to some understanding of our self.

The brain is three pounds of a jellylike material. But it, including the mind (which will be considered in more detail below), somehow becomes *us*. What we experience of the outside, what we feel on the inside, including what matters to us, our beliefs and hopes, seem to happen in here, in this organ. Despite the brain seeming so alien to us—it is *us*. The brain/mind makes us, *us*. Although this incredible physical organ in our body seems so unknown to us, sitting in its dark cave of the skull, the mystery of the brain/mind is that, somehow, it **is** us. It's amazing - and mysterious! All the brain/mind experiences, and functions, result in our being what we are. As the physical brain is always changing, so are we—we are a *work in progress*. When the tragedy of Alzheimer's disease occurs in its extreme form and the brain loses its normal functioning, it can be said of the person that he or she 'is with us but not at home'.

#

The brain is an unbelievable marvel of biology. Scientists tell us that one of the incredible features of the brain is the enormous number of cells it has: an estimated 170 billion. About 86 billion of these are electrical cells, called neurons. These are constantly communicating with one another—at a very rapid rate. They do so by using a combination of electrical and chemical signals. Thought, therefore, and all the brain's activities are a result of *material, physical* processes.

The brain's very basic function is to keep the body alive. Everything it does remains hidden from us, without our being aware of it. The brain makes decisions controlling the complex machinery of the body; for instance walking, breathing, swallowing. The brain/mind regulates heartbeat, blood pressure, and breathing. It is also responsible for hunger, sleep cycles, sex drive, and other emotions, perceptions and thoughts. All these go to affect behaviour.

#

As mentioned in Chapter 4, the brain/mind problem will be touched on now, but only briefly. The problem is left to the scientists, biologists, the psychologists to discuss more fully. In this study, therefore, whatever the scientific explanations of mind/brain relationship are, it is taken *experientially* that the mind is intimately related to and has a great influence on the brain.

What follows is a brief discussion on the scientific mystery, named the 'Hard Problem.' This will provide more background to this problem of 'mind': What kind of brain activity is it that creates conscious awareness? The difficulty is how this evidently *incorporeal, intangible* phenomenon of mind stems from a *corporeal, tangible physical* organ the brain? As mentioned above, all the brain's activities are a result of *material, physical* processes.

There are two main viewpoints put forward.
1. *Monist/materialist* viewpoint states that after the data, produced from eye impacts, say, enters the brain, it generates brain activity. This results itself, they say, in conscious perception. In this case consciousness is therefore part of the material universe. It is identical to the brain activity. It developed when awareness mechanisms evolved—but only as a result of these brain activities, rather than for any purpose of its own. So, it *appears* to be produced by certain types of *physical activity* in the brain. However, it is not known if, or how, despite many theories, this activity forms non-physical consciousness,
2, The D*ualist* viewpoint states that, say, after data produced from eye impact stimuli enters the brain, it generates brain activity. However, then the brain activity *allows* the mind to make conscious perception. Unlike the monists view, the brain does not itself generate conscious perception. In other words, consciousness is *non-physical* and exists in *another dimension* to the material universe. Although some dualists say there are certain brain tasks associated with, but not identical to, consciousness; other dualists believe consciousness may exist without the brain processes related with it at all. Some ask if the brain corresponds with a different thing altogether; this thing being what we call the *mind* or *consciousness*. If consciousness is not simply a result of brain activity it would suggest that the universe is:

just one aspect of reality, and that consciousness is part of
a parallel reality, in which entirely different rules apply.

Rene Descartes (1641) is regarded as being the founder of mind–

body dualism. His philosophical view of mind is that mental occurrences are non-physical, and thus non-spacial; that is that the mind and body are distinct and separable.

#

Where thought comes from and how it is created is of great interest. Much has been discovered about the brain/mind with the invention and the use of such things as brain scanners. Ever more detailed maps of the brain functions have been made through scanners such as PET, MRI and MEG.

#

Brain and psyche are related. As with brain/mind, they are related but distinct.   One can be aware of having two distinct types of consciousness. One being, outside, objective sense impacts. The other kind of experience the subjective, inner mind activities, such as thoughts and the other products of the mind. This mentation is the non-physical, non-spacial, experience, of the psyche.

So, what is the nature of mind? A thought or an idea or a feeling is quite a different kind of thing to anything else in the physical universe. Mind is not a thing; it occurs, it happens, it is a happening; it is an action, an activity. A concrete thing has material, it has mass. A thing is like a stone, whereas a happening is an event like a wave on the surface of the water. The mind is like a wave which is a happening between the wind and the water. It is not solid, not real, it is insubstantial. In our everyday life substantial things cannot simply dissolve into nothing. But insubstantial things, such as waves will just disappear, leaving no trace. It is an illusion, compared to the course of time, that a quantity of water is moving over the surface, whereas it is just moving up and down. Just so, a similar illusion is that there is 'self' moving through successive experiences, moving throughout life.

#

We seem to have a mind; it appears real to us. No action seems worse than one that is done, so called: 'mindlessly'. But can you say where your mind is located? Mind appears due to thoughts. But being a process, its perceived existence is due only to thoughts. The mind is therefore uncontrollable; to do so it would need to have a controller. One part of the mind would have to be controlling another part of the mind. There is nothing beyond the mind; there is no body to manage it. The contents of our minds have no location in either time or space. The mind, turned outwards, results in thoughts and objects. In the previous chapter, it was seen that thoughts enable us to construct symbols of things apart from the things themselves. This enables us to make symbols of ourselves, apart from ourselves. We learn to identify ourselves with the *idea* of ourselves. So, we have a subjective feeling that we have a 'self' which has a mind. This idea of 'self' is a reality to us, useful and valid, provided it is known for what it is, but calamitous if it is identified with our actual nature.

#

This seeming reality is what we name the 'ego.'
On waking up we start making decisions immediately; *we* are the 'captain of the ship'—*we* think. This is because on becoming awake/conscious we think that we are in control. But we are deceived. For there is a stowaway on board that is actually in control: but what or who is it? It is our brain or, more precisely, it is our brain/mind.[41]
One thing that we are conscious of is:
I AM.

But what is this self of which I am conscious? The more one considers it the more mysterious it becomes. The self, or ego, seems to be a changing series of material and psychological states. But despite 'I' being a seemingly changing entity, one has to begin with this statement: 'I exist' or 'I am.'

In the first place, is the creation of the 'ego,' our *seeming*, 'centre,' me? This centre refers to my psychological self. But is this my true *natural* self—my *true* 'me'? By understanding how our mind works, with its thoughts and feelings, its perceptions and so on, in other words, that is what the ego is, it may help in solving the enigma of who we really are.

As Alexander Pope was quoted as saying above:
Know then thyself, presume not God to scan;
The proper study of mankind is man.[42]

It is necessary to understand oneself before being able to make some effort at solving the problems that we have *within*, *without* and the consideration as to whether there is a *'Beyond'*.

#

We all experience the seeming fact of our existence; we are aware of, and conscious, of our own existence.

Our enquiry must therefore take consciousness as its first consideration. Again, this shows that the problem needs to have a *psychological* approach.

Consciousness is one of the outstanding scientific mysteries. Progress has been slow in trying to understand it. Is it possibly because the general conception of consciousness is wrong? Science seems to have difficulty with it as it cannot be measured or analysed. Some scientists find the existence of consciousness an insult to what they believe. However, many scientists now accept consciousness as a given, and seek to understand its relationship to the objective world.

There is much debate regarding the relationship between mind and consciousness. This study touches but lightly on the theoretical debate concerning this, but will consider the part consciousness plays in our lives more fully as it progresses.

#

The brain/mind brings about the *idea* of 'self.' From this idea we can 'verify' our experiences to be our own. This idea also relates both to our inner world, that is our thoughts and intentions, with our outer world with 'my' body and 'my' actions.

Referring to our three mysteries, Chapter 2, we divide the world into that which is *subjective,* our inner world, and that which is *objective,* our outer world. There is a boundary between the two. The boundary acts like a kind of 'holder' or 'receptacle,' which holds the subjective, inner world, inside and places our objective world outside. This holder we call the '*self.*' This self includes our thoughts, intentions, habits and so on. Under normal conditions all experiences include a sense of self, often unnoticed consciously. When the sense of self becomes conscious, we talk of being 'self-conscious.'

#

The brain supplies data *to* the mind, but it also receives data *from* the mind. The conjured-up data of the mind stimulates the brain more than the brain's own sensed data. In the brain/mind relationship, the brain is the instrument of the mind. It therefore carries out the the instructions of the mind. The result is that the sensed *percept* changes into a *concept.*

Should the mind interfer before the sense gathering is complete, which will normally happen because of the mind's speed of interference, there will be an incomplete perception, and the concept will be faulty. However, if the perception is full and free, there will be formed in the mind a true conception, *of that which is* sensed. Commonly the brain's response, or perception, to an incoming sensed impact is immediately affected by the mind's response to the impact. This produces an image which overlays the actual perception. This response itself depends on the kind of previous past experiences that the memory has stored, with reference to this particular perception.

The mind, from its own memory, reacts to the incoming data from the brain; interpreting these sense inputs reaching it. The interpretation depends, of course, on the psychological records that the mind's memory has kept. So, arrives, with the perception, this **self**, which is the Thinker, the Namer, the Enjoyer, the Censor, the Experiencer which is always thirsty for more experience, and so on.

#

It is the effects that the mind has on our lives, and how we can deal with them, that is a main concern in this study.

Most of our problems are to do with our not knowing who we really are, which may suggest that they are mainly psychological problems.

#

The mind produces the consciousness of self: *me*. The mind has an awareness that it, together with the whole body, is 'me, my-self'. It seems permanent; for you wake up in the morning and—immediately—there *you* are.

The brain's main function is the preservation and well-being of the whole organism—its prime concern is for the survival of the self, and for it to be happy.

For the self to function properly the *brain* indicates the need for sleep, produces the physical appetites of hunger, thirst and so on. The sexual desire ensures the continuation of the species. All creatures share these self-preservation instincts. It functions at this level on natural instinct.

#

However, the *mind* overlays the *natural*, biological *me* with a special, more powerful, kind of 'self': a psychological me. This mind-produced self—called the *ego*—is due to the brain/mind storing personal experiences of the past, sensations, perceptions and emotions. These together with the sub-conscious, inherited characteristics and the basic human instincts, help to build up the ego or centre of the self—they create my 'ego-I'.

We—which means all of humanity and possibly all living things—soon develop this sense of 'I' when young. This produces feelings that: "I am in control—or at the least, I want to be!" and "I am the centre of the universe; the world revolves around me."

#

The mind makes you (you inside) think that you are doing everything. You think that, in reality, 'you' are the instigator. 'You,' somewhere inside, is deciding what to do with the information. This is your reality. But actually, if you are not aware of it, it is not *you* that decides what to do with the information. The information, itself, takes over. That is—*unless* you are aware of it—*it* runs *you*.

Thought runs us by giving the false feeling that we are running it; *we* think that we are the ones who control our thoughts. In practice, unless we are aware of it, it is thought that controls each one of us.   And how much are we in control of our thoughts? For instance, do you know exactly what your next thought will be?

#

Take for example how we come to a decision:

D. Kahneman makes these closing comments in a programme entitled 'How You Really Make Decisions' (BBC February 2014)

"I think it is important, in general, to be aware of where belief comes from ... and if we think that we have reasons for what we believe, that is often a mistake. Our beliefs, our wishes and our hopes are not anchored always in reason; they are anchored in something else that comes from within and is different.

We have two systems of thought, which he labels as System 1 and System 2. Thinking System 2 is slow and sequential, as it requires effortful mental attention such as: What is 22 times 17? It is the system we think that *we* usually use. Thinking System 1 operates frequently, automatically and quickly with little effort or control on our part. This *intuitive* part of the mind is a lot more powerful than we realise. It affects many of our decisions, *'but we are stuck with our inner intuitive stranger.'* "By accepting it," he says, "we may come to a better understanding of our own minds."

This better understanding is a basic aim of the study.

#

Every decision we have made—a proposal, what to eat for dinner, what investment to make, whether to declare war and so on—our brain and minds have worked behind the scenes. Decision-making lies at the heart of everything in our lives— who we are, how we see the world, what we do. Before a decision is made there can be many competing drives all going on in the brain before a decision is made between these desires. For instance, the competing desire for a cake and the desire to lose weight. The brain/mind is constantly making decisions without our conscious help. 'How do we decide to decide?' By understanding how the brain/mind acts we can learn how to make better decisions for ourselves and society.

#

So, who do we *think* we are?

Images are formed and stored in the memory from the brain/mind sense impacts. Certain of these images collect together which identify themselves as 'me,' the observer; identifying as the self: 'me', 'mine'. They form together to protect and serve the interests of the self. These become the observer. The observer then observes the myriad of images which bombard the brain, which come from both inside - such things as thoughts and imaginations, and outside – from the senses. The observer can then make choices concerning the observed; liking and disliking. Thus, the ego is formed; the observer identifying as the 'self', 'me', 'mine.' This self seems very real to us. In fact, it does form our reality: 'I am.'. Nevertheless, as noted above, it is actually made up of images which are no different from the images that it observes. So, we see that the observer has separated itself from what is being observed. Despite this, the observer, this self, is fundamentally no different from the observed; both existing as ever-changing images of the mind.

Our personal consciousness[43] forms this impression: that there is an *observer, 'I'*, and an *observed, 'me'*. The observer and the observed *seem* separate. We seem to be fragmented into two parts. We seem to be a dual phenomenon. Once this image of *me* and *I* has been formed by thought in the mind, it seems that my *'I'* is the entity that is the creator of *my* thought. Thought seems to come from this image, 'I'. This 'I' is formed by thought itself. This production of an 'I' enables us to say, seemingly with great certainty: 'I am.' In this case the 'I' is the ego. In the personal consciousness of each individual human there is created the impression that there is an observer-me and an observed-you.

Our minds form an image that there is a thinker—who is the producer of thoughts. So, the thought and the thinker are the same, simultaneous mind activities. They are fragments from the same source.

Where there is a thought there is a thinker. And vice versa, there is a thinker ONLY when there is a thought. So:

> Where there is thought there is a thinker and
> 'I' becomes real in my own 'mind-produced world'.

There is a division between observer and observed. Without the object, the mind wouldn't sense anything; without the mind no object would be sensed—there would be no consciousness of it.
The observer and the observed are actually one conscious now-moment. In other words:

> the observer is the observed.

It is the mind, in this case, which is the source of our strong feeling of "I Am." It is stressed that this 'I' refers to my 'ego-I' or self.

Thought produces a centre from which I see my reality. This includes my relationships with my-self (my inner world) and with others and also my environment (my outer world). My own thoughts themselves, erupting from mind with its memory store, become my reality. The problem here is the fact that:

> Truth is not 'That Which Is Real to Me'.

#

If *I* did not name anything there would be no *me* who names. Conversely if there was no *me,* who names, there would be nothing named.

Where there exists a name, there is a 'namer.'

Where there is no *namer* there would be no "oak," just a tree; there would be no "tree," just a forest; there would be no "forest," just landscape; there would be no "landscape" just .... and so on—leading to the Whole of Nature and finally on to Truth: That Which Is—One and Indivisible[44].

It is essential that we live in this 'thought-divided' world. It has brought many benefits, but at the same time it is important to realise its limits.
Being aware of these limits, thought and thinking should be accepted, whatever they are and however they affect us—provided we are in control[45]. In other words, we should celebrate our humanness; warts and all!

#

This 'I' however thinks of itself as separate from its body: the 'me'.

Thus, we get 'my body, 'my head' and so on. This results in fragmenting the individual into a usually 'good' 'I' and an often naughty disobedient 'me'. So, we seem to have two selves: firstly, an *I*-self, the 'Observer.' And this self is seeing and influencing a second *me*-self—the Observed.

St. Paul saw it this way when he said:
> 'For what I do, is not the good that I want to do; no, the evil that I do not want to do—this I keep on doing. Now if I do what I do not want to do, it is no longer I who do it, but it is sin living in me that does it. ... I see another law at work in the members of my body, waging a war against the law of my mind ... What a wretched man I am! Who will rescue me?'   Romans 7:19-24

#

When one *sees* the truth of how thought operates, there is nothing to be done. If the truth of this is seen—the truth is realised, as a fact—then that is the end of it.

To see, for instance, that the idea of my self is false, is to discover the actual relationship between my inner and outer worlds. Relationships are important to understanding life; and these two, opposites, are particularly so.

Specifically, here, we have the opposites: my *inside (me)* and my *outside (my experience)*. A coin can be used as a metaphor. The two surfaces of the coin represent: my individual, illusory, inner self, on one side, and the outer world, on the other.
It is when we realise that *my idea of myself* is *not myself*, but is an illusion, then the distinction – the *subjective* distinction - between *me* and *my experience, is got rid of.* It is to see that these are both abstract limits between my inner and my outer – THAT WHICH lies between them is the concrete reality. It is THIS, which is the valuable coin itself. And THIS we have no words for; even though we know and are conscious of IT.

#

There is the question of the control of thought once this is realised. We are conditioned to believe that I—the thinker—am different from my thought. So, we say: 'I will control my thought'. The insight is: '*I, myself, am* the thought.' (*The thinker is the thought.*) But when one sees the truth that thought itself is 'me' and that it is thought that has created this—say, envy—then the truth concerning the observer being the observed is seen. It is seen not intellectually but through insight—and conflict ceases.

> As long as there is an observer, the experiencer, the thinker, there must be a division. Conflict ceases when the observer is the observed.

#

It is then possible to truly live KNOWING and thus feeling that we are whole—un-fragmented. When we feel that the experiencer is no different from the experience the two seem to coincide so that there is just *experiencing*. Likewise, the knower is no different from the knowing; the thinker is no different from the thought. It is all happening in the now-moment. The mirror reflects exactly that which is. One is fully conscious in that moment; the ego, the observer, is merged with the observed.

Thought, having the ability to construct symbols of things apart from the things themselves, creates a symbol, an idea of ourselves apart from ourselves. We learn to identify ourselves with the idea of ourselves. So, we have a 'self' which 'has' a mind, which, when the truth of this is realised, changes the relationship between subject and object, knower and known. The knower no longer feels it is standing apart from the experience. As a consequence, the seeking of 'getting something out of the experience of life,' becomes ridiculous.

#

We need to receive the gift of insight that me 'The Observer' is me 'The Observed'. No amount of intellectual theorising can bring about this realisation.

#

Jesus said: "Come unto me all you that labour and are heavily laden, and I will give you rest"[46]

In the world of today we can often feel 'heavily laden'. This must surely be referring not only to the stresses of working life, but more importantly, to the burden placed on us by our own mind-activities. These often 'drive' us[47]; they are the cause of our psychological burdens, especially the burden of our ego. It seems a truism, that the burden of carrying the *self* can be very heavy, if it is not carried lightly; that is: 'taking oneself lightly'.

Jesus claimed that he *had* the answer to – and *was* the answer to, and *is* the answer to - this burden. Is one reason for this because he himself experienced the love and joy of living in a certain dimension?

#

We see that your ego-I, the mind's 'I,' is very useful in many practical ways, but it is not a concrete actuality. It is just something that exists in the mind. One's intellectual 'I' is what it feels *now* at this moment. It can be acting totally differently a moment later—changing from moment to moment.

In this search for 'me' it seems more and more likely that:
> Our actors are melted into air, into thin air.
>
> Shakespeare's: The Tempest.

****

Further, we may also ask: What is it that observes the whole mind process of observer-observed—which we can call *Pure Awareness*, or *Pure Seeing*? The study's answer at this point is, as before, that it remains vague—a mystery. This is not saying that this study is a failure. It should not be considered a failure just because one cannot *name* it. It has been said that the name is not the thing itself:
> the description is not the described.

What the study has shown, if anything so far, is that one has to be very cautious when using the mind's constant desire to name. When you ask 'Who am I?', ask yourself: 'Who is asking this question?' It must come from inside you—the answer cannot come from outside. You can first of all think about it; philosophise about it. But if you do, you will be using the intellect and the answer will be from the outer periphery of your ego-self. This will bring you to realise that, yes, you are a self but this particular self must be something other than your ego-I. The mind, the intellect, will be able to ask the question, but it will never be able to provide the true answer—it will be unable to give any answer, other than theories, philosophies, guesses, or comforting hopes. The mind will never be able to come across the Truth. However, this outer layer of consciousness is not the only layer. We are able to go 'deeper' as it were.

#

Our inner world is made up of layers. We have the outer layer—the layer nearest the outside world—the brain which receives the senses from the outside and automatically responds through instinct. The next deeper layer is the mind, the intellect producing the ego. This can be called the 'periphery' of consciousness. It is rational and does the thinking.
But then there are further 'layers' of consciousness. Go deeper, beyond the mind, many say[48] *they* have discovered the seat of consciousness, the true self. This *'bottom of the soul'* is *claimed* by some to be our true self. It is witnessing continually.   It remains awake twenty-four hours a day and seven days a week, even when we are not aware of it. It is mirror-like. Until this is realised, it is as if you are standing with your back to it. You have only to turn—which is named 'repentance' *in Christian terms.*

If you are identified with the false ego, being on the periphery

—near the *outside*—you will be affected by every event from the outside. So, is it possible to become aware of another self, an innermost self, our true Self? If it is, it promises to provide answers? Of course, this must not be taken as true until it can be realised for oneself. This important question will be discussed in another chapter.

Jesus, in his discourse concerning the Counsellor Spirit[49], speaks to those who are identified with the ego, who are living on this periphery, and so are being affected by the changes and chances of this dimension.

He says to them:

> Peace I leave with you. My peace I give you. I do not give to you as the world gives. Do not let your hearts be troubled and do not be afraid.

John 14: 27

#

This wonderful organ, the brain/mind should be only for the *use of* humankind. There is no argument that it has produced incredibly wonderful achievements. But we see, in another sphere of life, that over and over again humankind has been, and is itself being, *used by* the brain/mind. It seems that it often drives *us*, rather than it being under our control. The brain/mind invariably *uses us*.

The brain/mind drives people to do incredibly brave, or conversely, stupid things. For instance, the mind often *drives* people to try to do things— literally mad things sometimes—well beyond what the physical body was designed to normally do.

Some people are proud to say: "I am driven to do *so and so*". But, do we recognise what it is that is doing the driving? Is it not our minds, themselves?

It is similar to Jesus' description of the Sabbath; as being made for humankind, not humankind for the Sabbath.

He said:

The Sabbath was made for man, not
man for the Sabbath.[50]

We are often seen to be the servant of the mind, rather
than it serving us. All our ideas of getting something
in the future, self-improvement, achieving some kind of
spiritual target, and so on, relates only to our illusory
image of ourselves. They give even more legitimacy to
the image when doing so.
So, what is our non-conceptual self?

#

Soon after birth with the development of the mind we
develop a personality, a persona. The origin of this term
is the mask worn by the Greek actors through which they
could play their parts and through a megaphone-like
trumpet make themselves better heard[51]. From this we
get the term 'person'[52].

'Self-ness' is another word for 'Personality.' Both refer to the
same consciousness of being, and also being a separate self.

Just as with the Hard Problem concerning the brain/mind
relationship, there is difficulty as to how you would describe the
nature of this *Personality* or *Selfness*. The two general views
given can be broadly summed up:

One is that within particular embodied selves, there are two
elements: psyche and body. (*'Psyche'* can be taken here to be
the totality of the human mind, conscious and unconscious.)
  Behind the perceptions resulting from the outer and inner
experiences, there exists some sort of 'soul' by which these
experiences are organised. In turn, this organised experience
turns into a particular and unique personality.

The other important view is that a person is a kind of a 'trinity:'

body, psyche and spirit.   The body and soul, or psyche, are related, but are not the same. Selfness/Personality is a product of these first two elements.   The body and the psyche are that which are being observed, experienced; they are not what observes or experiences. It is the spirit, the third element that is the observer or experiencer. The third element, being spirit, as will be discussed, is of similar character to, or even identical with, that which has been referred to as the 'Beyond.'

So, it is not surprising that the image that one presents to the world can change depending on the circumstances. It depends on *acting* at the time as a father or mother; daughter or son; wife or husband; employer or employee; teacher or student, and so on. We become a character. It is this *personality* which is felt to be important in society.

Being a character is sometimes likened to being a character acting on the world stage. As Shakespeare put it:

All the world's a stage,
And all the men and women merely players:
They have their exits and their entrances;
And one man in his time plays many parts,
His acts being seven ages.
As You Like: It Act 2, scene 7

#

All major religions, and those who are responsible for the upbringing of children, are against selfishness to any degree.

Sharing is one of the hardest things for a child to learn at first. It needs little analysis to see that the basic reason for much of the world's problems lie, not with Nature as it is, but with selfishness.

#

Attempting to positively rid ourselves of selfishness through some method or other, is as impossible to do as it is to defy nature's gravity and lift oneself up by pulling up on one's feet.

To enable one to deliberately lay plans—to become unselfish, be good or to be happy—means that the ego-I is intent upon results. These results are classed as being 'outside' like an object which may possibly be attained[53]. The ego-I seems to see these as being 'objects' outside of self—but of course they are not external objects; they are actually internal.

In conscious *self-effort*—in trying to achieve a goal, however idealistic or virtuous—the ego-I is basically striving for self-importance. In cultivating the good, aiming at consciously achieving happiness or achieving nirvana and so on, whatever it is, disappears when we look to see if we have attained it. Also, a change is not a real change, if it has a motive.

This is the gratification of the self, with its pretended realities, pursuing non-existent goals, and the future that never comes. All these show that, by having a motive to make the imagined 'better' future more important than where one is now, will be to miss the very point of life.

There is however the natural, freely given good for which no effort is required, as all possess it through our simply having been born.

#

Here the solution is in the problem itself. It is in the realisation that the *ego-I* is trying to gain or become something that it thinks would be desirable over *what is* now. This ego-I that thinks: "*I am; but this is not good enough—I want to be/have/do ...*"—is literally a product of thought.

It is the thought that produces the thought itself. 'I' am the thinker. *The thinker is the thought.* Without the thought there would be no thinker.

The observer becomes the observed.

If I realise, not only through the *intellect* but, through insight as a *fact*, that there is no *actual* 'ego-I' that I call myself, then the denial is brought about without effort or will-power.

The self is 'denied' by realising that it is not an *actuality* but exists only in the mind's *reality*—inside the head. However, it does need an *insight* with a resulting *realisation*[54] for this to become a reality to one.

This seems be an answer to the seemingly impossible command by Jesus:

> "If anyone would come after me, he
> must deny himself ...."
>
> Matt 16:24, Mark 8:34, Luke 9:23

#

A self-imposed property of the ego is that it *must* exist: it must be defended at all costs. It must be remembered that the ego-I is important in many ways to each of us. Just as the mind has its dangers, as pointed out in this study but nevertheless it is important to us, so it is with our ego. The point to remember is to be aware of the nature of our *internal world*. In this awareness, one is no longer ignorant of the mind's self, which is vice; this being Boethius' view.

The ego has a number of necessary, natural self-defense mechanisms. One of the main functions of the brain and its evolution is our survival. It is therefore natural that both fear and disbelief arise when one hears that the 'self' must be denied. That is: the centre of what we *think* is our true centre must be exploded, dropped or left behind. This is because the ego-I is the *centre of fear*. We have and always will have a mechanism to defend ourselves physically. This is activated by the brain/mind when a real (to the individual self) danger occurs. This is so even if only imagined and there is no actual physical danger present. We do not often, hopefully, have to face actual physical fear in our everyday lives. Examples of fear in everyday life for many may be in watching a thriller play, or hearing of someone's horrific injury and so on.

However, there is a greater fear to what may happen if our centre—our ego-I—is not 'denied' or 'left behind'. If it is thought about, this will be that we go on in the same old way with unfettered, mind-dominated selfishness and error.

Without realising who or what we really are will lead, yes, often to happiness or pleasure; but this can be only for a limited time. Ultimately, inevitably, it will also lead to frustration, unhappiness and suffering. This is inevitable, because, as discussed above, although it is *reality* to us, it is virtual in *actuality*. As quoted, this ignorance is a vice, for it is divorced from truth. Thus, it is found that all ideas of self-improvement are delusional.

In actuality, Nature or Truth will have the last word. Also, perhaps the greatest disaster, is that Love will be unable to flourish; for where the false ego is, Love cannot be.

The main difficulties concerning the ego is that it cannot come to Truth and, when present, cannot lead to Love.

Unlike Jesus, when he commanded: 'Get *behind* me Satan'[55], we cannot put our ego-I behind us by sheer desire or determination. But it can be put behind us, exploded or 'left behind.'

This particular product of the mind, the production of the ego, leads to enormous man-made suffering. This suffering can be in the form of saying a spiteful word, through anger and its effects, to what can only be termed 'wicked' or 'evil' selfish actions. These acts can be so appalling that we, as human beings, cannot feel responsible for them. So, in order to preserve our ego intact we place the responsibility for our actions on a convenient concept: the concept of Satan, who is the personification of evil. The mind, the producer of the ego-I, is very clever at making itself comfortable by blaming, in this case, an unholy spirit over what it has done! 'Satan, the Tempter' or the mind?

The basic Mind, however, free from the overlaying thinking mind that is being discussed here, seems to be the source of a 'Conscious Observer.'

#

So, what is the nature of this Conscious Observer? We know that it is not the ego-I. If it is thought that there is an Observer who is a permanent Self, we can ask: 'Where is this Observer located?'   One can see that, wherever one thinks this centre of consciousness is located, you have to ask: From where is *this* place being observed?' If the answer is 'We feel that it is behind the eyes or the solar plexus,' this observation must come from some other point of observation. But where is this? Then we go on: where is this? We can continue asking this until - actually it is quite soon - we get to a point where it is realised that the place of observation is unknown

—seemingly *unknowable by the mind*. The mind would want to name it, but to name it requires the thinking mind. It is this thought that separates us from the actuality of purely 'seeing'.

It is easy to be tempted into giving explanations of this, and of course many try to do so. The explanation by those who have had this experience, in which self is not, depends upon their background: their culture, language, religion and so on. Thus, there are many explanations —usually religious. Examples are given at the end of Chapter 8.

#

The subject of this chapter has been mainly to get to know what one normally considers to be one's self—in this case the ego-self with its ever-changing nature.

This identity, called the ego or self, although due only to an image formed in the mind, need not cause problems provided that we are aware that it only exists in our individual reality[56]—that is in our mind only and does not actually exist in truth. It is real enough in our home-made, mind world.

Naturally in everyday life our sense of ego is very useful and important to us. The ego will naturally develop very early in our conventional life and we will always know that the mind will give us self-awareness —awareness that we are specific body-mind individuals. 'Self-esteem' (*amour-propre*) is an important factor in a person's psychological make-up. However, as we know, this ego is usually taken very seriously and—in wrongly thinking it more real than actuality itself—leads to enormous suffering. This resulting suffering will be both to the individual whose ego it is and, quite often, to others who come within its influence.

Repeating the earlier question, referring to my 'ego', my *seeming psychological centre*: Is this my true *natural* self, my *true* 'me'?   When we realise that the answer is 'No,' that the ego-I is a false mind-made self, we do not disappear in a puff of smoke! We still feel and know that: 'I AM'. So, maybe, we could ask, not only "Who am I?' but 'What am I?'

So, there must be another 'I' which has been screened 'behind' one's, ever-changing, ego-I. This other 'I' must exist in order for there to be preserved this basic knowledge: '*I AM*'. The nature of this other 'self' will be enquired into later in the study.

However now it is asked: what other world, or dimension, can we live in?   These two worlds, or dimensions in which we can live will be contrasted in the next chapter.

6 - OUR TWO WORLDS

From the last two chapters it can be seen that we actually live in a 'home-made' world of our minds. Thoughts constantly stream through our heads. But is there another possible world, or dimension, other than this?

Throughout history people have reported exceptional experiences when certain conditions prevail. These can occur spontaneously, such as when overawed by some form of beauty or through, say, a sudden overpowering shock. It seems that they have come into contact with the 'given' world. This is the world of Nature which is the *actual* world. The experience is sometimes called 'mystical'.

#

It should be realised now that I cannot describe this 'given' world because *the description is not the described*. Words about the thing is not *the* thing itself.

So, there is no teacher or guru allowed here. The only way to discover the truth is to attend to the 'pointing finger' and see to what it points and thus find out for oneself, rather than believe what others tell you.

#

The world we habitually inhabit is the world of our mind.

The world of our mind divorces us, to a greater or less extent, from our contact with the 'actual' present world. Referring to the words of an eminent psychologist "The remembering self creates our reality more than our present-experiencing self." It takes but a brief time to realise that we tend to care more for our remembering self than for our experiencing self, which is our 'self-at-this-moment' in time.

Because of this Aldous Huxley called it our 'home-made world'.

#

For convenience I am going to coin two terms. These will act as a short-hand in this study.

Firstly, I will refer to the mode of consciousness when we are in the conventional, everyday mode of living—the ordinary, straightforward everyday experience - as living in the **A-Mode of consciousness**.[57]

#

When our minds are in the A-mode, the abstract or virtual nature of words divorces us, to some degree, from life. This is the world as experienced by the mind. The mind works using symbols, and in using the mind we experience the world by Analogy[58].

#

As set out in the rules for the approach to this study in Chapter 3, we need not necessarily change things as they stand but we should be *aware* of this abstraction: that it exists only in the mind.

#

Religion represents, or is an analogy of, the truth. These tenets of our various religious beliefs, even the specialist clothing, behaviour and hair styles, need to be understood (to be stood *under)* in order to see the underlying truth, if any, that they represent. What we should not believe is that any religion—its creeds, cults and ceremony, its statements in words—is THE Truth. It is not IT although it may represent it to a more or less extent.

This may seem like splitting hairs, but it is important to see the true concern of religion.Religion, as it is usually practiced, is concerned with either the past or the future. With the past: that is for forgiveness for doing or not doing things. With the future: that is for the hope of everlasting life in heaven or similar hope. However, 'true' religion should be concerned with **LIFE**. As 'life' occurs only in the present, religion should be concerned with the present.

#

So we can live in two 'worlds' or dimensions. Huxley writes that we are like amphibians, living simultaneously in:
  the **given**, or **real**, world which is the world of life and matter
    and
        the **world of symbols**, which is the world of the
          mind: that is our 'home-made' world.

We cannot live without symbolism in language and thought. These are needed in order to form concepts and to explain and communicate our life experience. But in this other world, or dimension, symbols are done away with.

#

Secondly then, I am adopting for brevity, when referring to this experiencing of the *given*, or *real* world, the term **Primary Mode, or P-Mode of consciousness.**
In this mode there is no concern with words or theories about reality. Its concern is with having a direct living grasp of existence itself.

#

There is no abstract symbolism in this P-Mode of consciousness. There is no naming by the mind. Functions of the mind, in the form of symbols, such as thoughts, imaginings, naming and so on, disappear.
Thought, which itself is always of the past, plays no part. The brain experiences the actuality of *that which is*, directly.
This mode of consciousness can only take place in the present moment, in the *Here and Now*. Thought cannot experience the present moment; it can think only of the past or imagine the future.

Paul seemed to refer to the difference between these two modes of consciousness when he writes:
> 'the letter kills but the spirit gives life.'
>
> 2Cor 3:6

#

As shared with other religions, Christian dogma is a symbolism, or an analogy, of experience arising from primary consciousness; often called 'spiritual experience.' This seems to be a shared experience; shared by people everywhere and throughout history.

#

***Primary* experiencing** takes place when in the P-Mode of consciousness. This state of consciousness is not a product of the mind's imagination or thought. Imagination and thought take place in the A–Mode and need time.
Life can only be fully *lived* when in the actuality of this present moment. One can only **be**, when in this P-mode of experiencing.

#

Glass has been used as an analogy to illustrate the two basic modes of consciousness.

One illustration of the A-mode of consciousness is a painting depicting a sunset on a stained-glass window. This is the result of an action derived from the mind of the painter. But, however well it is painted, it is static and will be nothing as compared to seeing an actual sunset through the plain glass of a window.

The painting will be fixed; it will be an image of the past. The metaphor used refers to river water, having been caught in a bucket, becomes just stagnant water.

A person will be—however briefly—in the second type of consciousness, now being called the P-Mode, if he or she perceives the actual sunset without the interference of naming or conceptualising it.

The following illustrate, using glass again as an example, the difference between these two modes of consciousness. The first illustration, showing the difference between the two modes of consciousness using glass, asks you to imagine focusing your eyes on the drops of rainwater running down a window pane; or perhaps on a pattern, say a floral design, etched into a pane of glass.

When focusing in this way the scene outside the glass is blurred, indistinct or it may even be unseen. This illustrates the A-Mode of consciousness.

If at the same time you see your reflection in the glass, it can refer to your ego-*self* which is 'in the picture' also.

Now if you refocus your eyes through the glass you will see what is actually there.
You will see the actual beautiful flower garden beyond.

This looking through the glass at the actual garden and s*eeing*, purely without naming what is seen beyond the pane of glass, illustrates the P-Mode.

'Looking on glass'—which under certain light, can also produce an image or reflection of the person looking as in a mirror—is a good analogy for this experiencing.

This idea is expressed in a verse of a hymn, written by George Herbert. The hymn - beginning with the first line *Teach me my God and King* - describes these kinds of experience:

> A man that looks on glass / On it may stay his eye,
> Or if he pleases / Through it pass, and
> then the heavens espy.

Paul also used this 'glass' analogy when he wrote:
> 'Now we see in a glass darkly, but then face to face,
> Now I know in part but then I shall know even as I am known.'
>
> 1 Cor 13:

#

Science also does not escape the fact that its formulas and theorems are not actually *true*. The expression 'not true' here being used in the sense that they are not *present actuality*. Formulas and theorems are symbolic and so only symbolise truth. The mystery is how, say, mathematical formulae can model the real world so closely; so closely that a ship or a plane can be designed on a computer with every confidence it will function as planned. The working of the mind or brain itself is marvelous. We can think, but we cannot say how we think, any more than we can explain how we actually see. 'I cannot tell you how I see. I can say I need to open my eyes; but even then, how do I open my eyes? I just can, and indeed do—it is natural.' We are using the mind all the time but the brain keeps us in the dark as to how it is functioning in order to produce what we experience inside us, thoughts, and what is outside, our world and universe.

#

Our minds are very good at solving problems of everyday life which need time to solve; problems we could name as 'outside' problems.

Our minds are not so good at trying to solve the problems of our 'inner' life—our psychological problems. Nevertheless, we try to solve these psychological problems by conscious-thinking rather than relying on that mysterious power, called by many names, one of which is the 'age-old natural wisdom of the body'.

'Living in the mind,' that is in the A-mode of consciousness, can be called living 'in the dark' when it is applied to the inner life —even to 'asleep' or even 'dead'! Such extreme language can be understood when comparing the quality of life between these two modes.
This is because we are closed in on our home-made world of the mind, which can be filled with the past and the future—for thought can never contact us with the actual present. When we are thinking we are necessarily thinking *in* the present, but the thinking itself is a result of time which is *of* the past.

Using the intellect properly is when one is solving 'outside' problems. One is living on the surface; for life of the mind is relatively superficial. This is perfectly good to do so. It can give pleasure and satisfaction, but remains on the outside. Psychologically it can be thought of as living 'horizontally'— travelling on a superficial level of consciousness in the world of thought[59].

Conversely when we are living in the open P-mode we are truly awake or alive. We are not veiled off from the *real-given* world by our mind's image coverings; these image coverings being things like naming, thoughts, memories from the past and so on. So here in the P-mode we are said to be living 'in the light'; we are travelling 'vertically'—inwards to ever deeper levels.

#

In order to discuss the approach to truth we need firstly to communicate through words, abstractly. This is the case in this study. It is in this respect that those religions that seek to know and describe the Truth, are *analogies* of the Truth.

Where the horizontal and the vertical meet, in the middle of the cross, is where life is in balance.

#

It is not wrong to make analogy or interpretation. A particular theological explanation may indeed have served humankind as a whole, or a society over a particular time in history, very well. In time certain interpretations will need to be questioned and maybe changed in the light of experience. This has been shown to be the case in Christian theology throughout its two-thousand-year history.

Some examples are:

- *the struggle to answer the question 'What was the nature of Jesus—Who do you say I am?'*
- *the resistance to scientific fact that, for instance, the world is not at the centre of the universe*
- *the theory of evolution versus creationism.*
- *the claim that a particular nation or group of believers are the 'chosen of God'; to the exclusion of others.*[60]

#

It has been stated that Life is a process which can have three main stages.

The first stage is the baby stage when things are seen as they are. It sees what is called the *given* world. A 'tree' is not seen. There is no concept, or idea, of *tree*. The baby's senses communicate directly with the brain, experiencing the whole moment fully. Babies have, in so far as their senses are developed, clear unmodified perceptions of the world around them. So they experience at the level of Primary consciousness, the P-mode.

The second stage occurs as the maturing child's neurons in the brain start to grow and make connections. Memory develops, for instance. Development continues into the adult stage. Quite quickly concepts are formed in the mind. Concepts progress from the more general (the recognition of parent as opposed to friend) to the specific concepts : *oak* as opposed to the *ash*, *sandwich tern* as opposed to a *little tern* and so on. In this stage people rarely see things fully as they really are. We are now in the world of symbols, such as names. This is the world of the mind: our 'home-made' world, referred above to as the Analogical or the A-mode.

#

It is at this point that the mature person's mind itself can be seen quite often *to use* the person; rather than the other way around. We generally do not realise this because we are not aware of what is actually going on 'below' the actual content of thought. The thoughts themselves are what we are aware of and overlay the actual.

In a third stage, a person, besides using the mind necessarily in the A-mode in order to communicate, may return to experiencing in a manner which is similar to that of the first stage: being aware with the mind in the P-mode of consciousness. As will be seen, this is a deliberate form of meditation. This stage may rarely, if ever, occur naturally, spontaneously, in one's life. Even if it does, it may not be recognised for the importance that it has. But many do experience, even if briefly, when heightened consciousness is triggered, the *given* world as it is. Sometimes one can act immediately without thought; often this happens in an emergency. This mysterious, seemingly natural, power intervenes. This kind of experience will be discussed in more detail later.

So in this third stage, when we are in the P-mode, we can again see things as they are, without the interference of naming carried out by the mind. With the thought processes stilled and by looking without naming, the thing perceived, or the feeling felt, is experienced as *it is*. No thought is there to give one a false perception.

There is a difference between the first and the third P-mode stages, although they do seem similar. The difference between the mature third stage and the childish first stage, is that, when something goes wrong in the third stage, we do not go running to mummy for comfort!

This changing process, which occurs in life and is due to the influence of our mind, could be what Jesus was referring to when he said:

"I tell you the truth, anyone who will not receive the kingdom of God as a little child will never enter it"?

Luke 18:17

#

Language is thus a code. We need to know the code's meanings. We can look at the writings of the New Testament and perhaps 'interpret' the reality behind the writer's 'coded' messages— finding a deeper meaning to them in the light of this study's findings. The writers interpretations of their actual experience would have been influenced by the kind of conventional thinking, or concepts, of the times that they were in. We need to look at their interpretation in the light of what we know today. After two thousand years much more is known through the manifold and diverse experiences of humanity.

#

The reason for our frustration, pain and unhappiness could be the result of our minds unremittingly pushing us (along the horizontal path)—to the neglect of the present. It pushes us not only now—as we seem to be continually struggling to achieve or acquire through the ego's relentless discontent—but to consider the future which is a pure abstraction *psychologically.* These are not necessarily unhealthy—it depends on the direction of their flow in relation to life's natural flow. Thus, for instance, fear is unnecessarily felt when thought makes us aware of our inevitable death—even though it is not present at this present moment. Thought introduces fear when there is actually the possibility of joy at this moment.

We hope for a better future, gradually working toward it. "It takes time" we say. Of course this is the case when learning to earn one's living, or practicing a sport or the piano; we are not referring to that kind of time which is called *chronological time.* We refer in this study only to our mind's attitude, that is our psychological condition, in which the future is a construct of the mind. Time in this context is called *psychological* time.

Chronological time is time as measured by a clock. Clocks are not only useful but are now essential to life. Without clocks and, more ominously now, without computers and internet devices our 'brainy' culture and lifestyle would collapse.

#

Chronological time is reliable because of the regularity of nature. It took a long time *(pun not intended!)* in order to construct a fairly reliable pendulum clock. (Thanks for this discovery go to Galileo.) *Chronological time* is based upon the regularity that is found in nature. If there was no regularity, and things just jumped around haphazardly, it would be impossible for there to be chronological clock-time. We discovered from nature that certain things follow on in a regular order. If this were not so we would not have such a thing as chronological time and all would be chaotic. This is how we obtain our, so called, physical 'laws'. This word 'law' is a misnomer as nature itself is not governed by laws as we know them; there is no legislature laying down how nature has to behave. There is no lawmaker behind nature; that is as far as science can prove. It has been found that there are regularities in natural occurrences. So we can produce 'laws' which can be used to our advantage. We call these 'necessary' laws for we are confident in their regularity of proceeding. So we are confident that a certain time tomorrow will be five o'clock. The natural regular pendulum swing of a clock can be relied upon.

However *psychological* time is much less assured. Psychological time has no 'necessary' order of following.

We cannot be very sure of what exactly went on in the past; and certainly not of the future. We may want to use psychological time to attain some desired outcome; many spiritual exercises try to do this. The fact is that the steps required to arrive at the desired *psychological* outcome are not of a necessary sequence; unlike one based on a scientific law. It may be possible for the psychological (or mind-driven) desire to be achieved, but it is usually very uncertain.

Psychological time is a product of the mind; it occurs when we are in the A-mode. It is created by thought. It creates a *distance* between what is and what 'I wish it to be.' Psychological time is required when I feel insecure and I wish to become secure after doing x, y or z. Of course we do need to have time to learn mathematics or painting, but this requires chronological time.

Every thought assumes time. We always think that everything, including thought itself, exists in time. This is time as we experience it. This is correct if *the order of succession can be put in terms of time.*

#

Psychological time is very unreliable. When bored, a minute will seem like an hour; but when interested an hour flies by like a minute.

We experience time as if we are moving from the past towards the future. But this makes no sense because the *psychological* future is non-existent; so this analogy of the future spread out before us is incorrect. Similarly we can say the similar thing of the past. It is only the present that exists.

The *psychological* fact is that there is only the present—the **Now**.

#

So time is the *virtual representation* which follows the fact that there is an orderly flow or stream of consciousness.
Our idea of time has been influenced by thought.
All thought involves time in a way that is not noticed. We think that everything exists in time and that time is an independent reality. However, by illustration, we can use a distance/time graph with time drawn as a horizontal line. A point on the graph represents a point in time. This is then followed by another point, then another and so on. The line of the graph is a series of infinitely small points. These points on the time line, in other words, represent a *succession* of points. Thought represents these points through space. This space represents time which represents the order of successive existence. It is the order of *succession*.[61]

#

So time is actually based on the succession in which things succeed each other in a certain order.

Time is a concept. This concept, which is created by thought, *represents* succession. The actual thing is **That Which Is**: a succession of events.

There are many examples of succession, such as the phases of the moon, the four seasons. These are the succession of process. The body goes through a succession of rhythms. All these things rest on succession.

#

  When we are in the P-mode we are conscious of the present. The brain's pure perceptions have no regard to past or future, but only of the Present—the *Eternal Now*.
The more you anticipate the future the more you miss the Now-moment. The more we look to the future with its imaginative promises the more we miss life; largely unconscious of the happiness and beauty of the Moment.

#

The brain can foresee the future, especially the certainty of death. The brain/mind, in which the egotistic mind is formed and resides, desires everlasting existence. Will death be so terrible? The physical pains of it and the psychological pains of parting may obviously be awful. But after a hard day's work the sensation of falling into unconsciousness can be very pleasing.

#

The basic perceptions of the brain know actuality directly rather than ideas about it. This is "primary consciousness" which we have been calling the P-mode of consciousness. It lives completely in the present, and perceives nothing more than what is at this now-moment. In this mode of consciousness there is no past and no future, no motive or desire to be—one **is**.

Everything that happens in the brain happens in the present. If one lets go, letting the brain naturally function without self-interference, there will be a spontaneous natural response to the situation. This effortlessly going with the flow will bring peace and calmness into everyday life.

It is possible that **Insight** into a problem can lead to immediate change without the effort of the self trying to solve the problem.

#

Each of the modes of consciousness has a strong connection with the environment. The A-mode has a strong connection with man-made, mind-made environment. The P-mode has a strong connection with the **Natural** environment.

A major cause of people's poor functioning in the West shown by the breakdown in relationships, drug use, drunkenness, selfishness, greed, material excesses and so on must be ascribed to this alienation from the Natural world.

A person living enclosed by the man-made world, whose mind is dominated by man-made thoughts through the use of technology, such as television, radios, mobile phones, computers and the internet, has little chance of escaping the A-mode of consciousness. We are unbalanced in this respect. We need to regain a proper balance between the A and the P modes.

St. Bernard, who created a rule followed by certain monastic institutions, taught that you will find in woods something you will never find in books. He said that:

> *'Stones and trees will teach you a lesson you never heard from school teachers.'*

#

Can we learn from just looking at something natural,
such as a tree? Can we become aware of the tree;
particularly being aware of its stillness: its **'being'**.

#

One motive for carrying out this study was to see why, despite the fact that most people desire peace, we continually have wars.[62] We say: 'We must learn from this terrible needless suffering caused by this (latest) war; and we must never go to war again.' We endlessly repeat this. This is an example of thought moving along the 'horizontal' path causing problems which it cannot resolve—except perhaps a temporary sticking plaster—producing a self which creates identification, 'us and them' competition and so on—and then trying to solve its self-created problem. However the thing—in this case a certain aspect of the mind—that causes the problem can never resolve it completely by itself.

When we see that the behaviour of humanity cannot be changed by using thought alone—nor by attempting to impose a solution from the outside—we will find that truth will lead us to realise that change can only take place from within; that is on the inside, psychologically. That is why the only person you can change is yourself.

Only when we can enter the dimension of the 'given world,' balancing our 'home-made world,' will we find peace—for the individual first and then, as it consists only of individuals, society.

#

This chapter has considered approaching the possibility of a 'Beyond'—in two ways. One which uses mentation, and the other by using immediate or direct experience.

The former imposes an order and meaning on the 'Beyond' by attempting to describe it.

The latter can be illustrated by the experience of:
> *"hearing the sound of the Lord God*
> *as he was walking in the garden in the cool of the day."*
>
> Genesis 3:8

That is having a direct experience with the divine.

Thought produces theological beliefs whereas spiritual experience comes from a source other than thought.

#

The questions again come naturally: 'If there is this *given world,* how is it entered?' and 'What is this source of spiritual experience?'

These will be looked at in the next chapters, 7 and 8 respectively.

> > > >

PART TWO - ON THE WAY!

7 - AWARENESS

At the end of the last chapter, it was stated that life can only be fully *lived* when in the actuality of this present moment. One can only **BE** when in this P-mode of experiencing. So the question was asked: 'If there is this *given world,* how is it entered?'

This seeking to satisfy the mystery at the depth of our very being—answering the question 'Who Am I?'—as has been seen, cannot be made through any kind of mentation, thinking or reasoning. Because of this, silence needs to be brought to the mind. So in order for thoughts to dissolve away, we must look at the mode of consciousness which takes place in the silence of the mind.

#

The mind cannot use the mind to silence the mind. We often begin our seeking to discover the truth by means of mind control: through concentration. Concentration is necessary in many mind-operations. We need to concentrate in most A-mode conscious operations, such as making a machine part, painting a picture, adding up a column of numbers and so on. It is used when there is a technique to be followed. Concentration, as a technique, is able to offer some mind-control. For instance, in yoga, concentration can be used as a step that will lead on to meditation, then on to contemplation. However, this control of the mind using concentration alone, valuable as it is, is limited usually to around the period of time that the effort is used. But once we slacken the effort to quieten our thoughts, we find that we are again deluged by a tide of these very thoughts.

 Referring back to the psychologist's words in Chapter 6: "The remembering self creates our reality more than our present-experiencing self,' we tend to care more for our remembering self than for our experiencing self, which is our 'self-at-this-moment' in time. The chapter described our *two worlds* in which we live. For the experiencing of the *given* or *actual* world—rather than our 'homemade' A-mode produced world—the term 'P-mode' of consciousness was coined.

Interestingly, there have been numbers of men and women, throughout the West as well as the East and throughout time, who declare that they have experienced and appreciated this state of Primary, or Pure, consciousness: the P-mode of consciousness. They have found it needful to be in the Here and Now; that is in a **state of awareness** in order to come across fundamental Truth. But we must not take their (positive) word for it. Anyone with the motivation to do so can look into this state, or dimension, for her or himself.
So if we seem to live in a home-made world of the mind, what is this other, *given,* world: is it accessible and, if so, how can we enter it? In other words, how can one wake up?

#

Awareness—meaning to have one's consciousness alive to the present actuality—can occur *involuntarily*, or naturally, as when one is suddenly confronted by an extraordinary sight such as a dazzling sunset. You become alive and awake, that is conscious, to the present reality. This awareness enables your *being* in the present.

This awareness can occur also *voluntarily* when one realises that, for example one's mind is absorbed with some kind of thought —one is 'asleep,' absorbed in a homemade world. This change is not an evolutionary gradual move; it is immediate. The transition is sudden. There is no effort involved. So there is no method that can 'force' this to occur. This consciousness cannot be forced, it is freely given; it is a grace. However as mentioned above, the 'window, or door, needs to be open for the wind to naturally blow in.'

#

In awareness, which consists of an observation without censure or identification, there is a conscious happening. Like the effect of a light being switched on; it is 'enlightening'. No mentation, mind activity, influences this observation. In this present awareness there is peace and being.

By watching yourself, without any identification, comparison, or condemnation - just watching - wonderful enlightenment occurs. Unconscious activity comes to an end and awareness of behaviour becomes apparent: activities are clear. However, this self-awareness is not to be confused with being introspective. It is quite the contrary: for this illusory 'self' needs no encouraging through the A-mode of self-absorption, self-observation or self-analysis. Through awareness this self is quietly disregarded. Awareness has nothing to do with self-improvement or the pursuit of an objective. Quite the opposite: it is the ending of the imagined 'I'. Awareness has no objective, no wish to attain. The lack of mental activity means the illusory ego-I is absent.

As an example: without verbally describing it, become aware of your present feeling now. If you do not name the feeling, that is with no verbalisation, but just by watching yourself, at that moment *you* are not. There is only a condition of being

—essential nature, actuality. But immediately you name the feeling you create an observer, who is the experiencer, and an observed, which is experienced. By being silently aware of the feeling, there is no separate-observer and no separate-observed; no dual joint phenomena. In a state of passive awareness, the observer is in communion with the observed; the two become one. The observer is the observed. There is no separate self; the image of the self 'merges' with the image of the observed. So, there is no *experiencer*. There is then, in the moment, only the being of experiencing. This can then become, later in memory, an experience.

Awareness enables the truth, the simple truth of everyday experience, to come into being. This is **being here, now**. The alert awareness of this present starting point is necessary before we can go far. We must begin near before we can go far. However, we find, between the start and the finish, that there is no distance to go: the beginning and the end are one.

#

As stated, in Chapter 5 , conflict ceases when the observer is the observed.
When we feel that the experiencer is no different from the experience it is then possible to truly live *knowing* and thus feeling that we are whole—no longer fragmented. The two, the observer and the observed, seem to be one-whole; so that there is just *experiencing*. Likewise the knower is no different from the knowing; the thinker is no different from the thought. The knower, the known and the knowledge are one.
It is all happening in the now-moment. The mirror reflects exactly that which is. One is fully conscious in that moment.

An important factor in this particular kind of attention or awareness is that there is no 'ego-I' present, which, as discussed in Chapter 5, is the product of the mind.
The thinking mind, that creates the ego-I, plays no part in

this; it is pure consciousness. It can be here that insight[64] or intuition can come into play—the brain's natural wisdom. When the brain/mind has this attention it will be in the true P-mode of consciousness. There will be an attending to 'What Is'. That is: attending to the *now*-moment, or the *attended*-moment.

In this most important moment the brain/mind is like a mirror. It receives an object—by way of sensing an outside object or an inner-mind object such as a thought—but it does not keep it. There is no motive and no energy expended when attending to 'What Is'.

#

We do use effort when in the everyday A-mode of consciousness. This consciousness is mental activity—we have to 'pay' attention. It is our 'everyday' mode; it is the film of the action of life which is projected onto the screen of our consciousness. This A-mode of consciousness is the attention necessary when living our life. In the case of 'paying attention' there is a limited amount of payment (or effort) that one can make over any period of time. It is useful, for instance, to have a break after driving for some time; as it is also to rest, every so often, when studying.

When it comes to living our inner/mind life—the desire to come across truth, say—the psychological struggle needs to be understood. Effort is used when a psychological struggle is made to change *What Is* into something else: *What Should Become*. The relationship, between the sensed data (person, idea, or object) and the mind that receives this data, is important. This relationship must be immediate. There can be no mediation of any kind in order for the truth, or actuality, to exist in consciousness. The ego-I mode of consciousness comes to an end; comes to an end happily and voluntarily without any hope of award. The ego-I mode produced by the mind of the *experiencer* must come to an end; the mode of the *chooser* must come to an end; the mode of the *observer* must come to an end; the will of the *achiever*[65] must come to an end. The seeker ceases. This can be named, using that much used word, 'meditation'.

The silence of the mind cannot be brought about through the action of the will. There is the saying: 'Where there's a will there's a way.' But the will, issuing as it does from the mind, cannot be used in this, psychological, situation. There must be no effort.
So what to do?

#

In this study awareness is a consciousness of naturally, effortlessly, **being** in the present moment: **now**.

There is no technique involved. In other words, we never need to ask *how* to be aware; it is a natural process of the mind. We are dealing with consciousness here and we must remember that consciousness is a gift—it is the very fundamental essence of our life. Consciousness itself, it has been said is a great mystery. Scientists have not explained it adequately. Appendix C discusses this further.
But one does not need to have a scientific qualification to know from our very experience of 'I AM' that it is an unearned, precious gift. In fact it needs just a little experience of the magic of this world, this universe, called 'creation', to know that consciousness is embedded throughout it—consciousness is cosmic.

#

In order to avoid this effortful attention to attain this natural or conventional awareness, the secret is not to try positively to see what to do or ask how to become aware. Simply, one just does it.   BUT having said that, it must be stressed that this awareness is based on the natural or conventional awareness in which the brain/mind functions naturally; using the senses for its security. This is the awareness that one has when in the everyday A-mode of consciousness. As has been discussed, this is the condition when living in our homemade world. But our homemade reality is not enough to fulfil the conditions of the experiencing the truth of the factual, given world. In Chapter 5, it was said that the mind influences the result of factual impacts of our senses. It does this by intervening in the data reaching the brain. The comment was that: *It is the effects that the mind has on our lives, and how we can deal with them, that is a major concern of this study.*

#

Now here is the thing.   Approaching the end of chapter 4 it was said: We rarely experience naturally living in the 'given' world—the world as it actually is. This *living in the actual world* implies living in the Now, in the Present.   It is because of the need to live in the Present that we need a consciousness which prevents, or nullifies, thought; thought which is always of the past.

But we know that we cannot influence our thoughts through using thought, so the need is to cut link between the BRAIN factual data and the MIND psychological data.   That is: the sensed factual - inner and outer - data must not be corrupted. This is done by having a 'negative' mind. A negative mind is not a blank one, but one which makes no psychological interference: no identification, no thought.   This is achieved by being 'choiceless'.   There is no ego making likes or dislikes; for it is a misconception that what is pleasant or good can be quickly seized from what is painful or evil.

As Seng-ts'an said: *The GREAT Way is not difficult, for those who have no preferences. Let go of longing and aversion, and it reveals itself.*

Here we look at life in its totality: we look at, say, happiness and sadness together. There is never one without its opposite; as with life and death together - they always go together. By so doing, what is there to choose? Realising that neither love nor hate, say, could exist without the other - they being ultimately one - choosing is not an option. There is no effort in this letting go. We no longer face one way.

#

In the early stages of coming across awareness, as described in this study, a phrase like: '**Now, Here, This**,' may well act as a reminder to oneself when in the A-mode to wake up from 'sleep.' (This expression *sounds* like a ship captain's command over the ship's intercom. It calls for the crew to listen to the coming notice: *'Now, Hear, This. Now, Hear, This.'*)

For always **IT** is **NOW;**
           I am always **HERE;**
         and I am (at one with) **THIS**.

But remember that this is still in the A-mode. Just the realisation that one is not in the P-mode—not in the present moment —brings awareness. Words are not needed to bring about awareness, or consciousness; this being a natural process. In fact words are a stumbling block.

Initially, many find that the experiencing of breathing is a fitting way to move into the present *now*—you awaken to the present by experiencing your natural in/out breathing— aware of the experiencing of the in/out breath through the nose There are to be no words; no counting, no naming; for this would continue to be in the A-mode. One needs only to be consciousness of either one or more of the body's sensations. Only one sensation now-moment can occur at a time, but as these occur sequentially at speeds which we cannot sense, they can seem to be occurring together.

These sensations can include, besides an awareness of one's breathing, the body's position, feelings, sensations, emotions, moods; movements, walking, sitting, rising from the chair. In summary: aware of all the impacts received by the brain with no psychological mind influence—no-mind. At these moments one's consciousness will be in the P-mode. As there is no verbalisation, there should be no naming. So, there will be the dropping of thought, which includes the use of 'I', 'me', 'my' and 'mine'. If any 'reminding' thought has to be used initially, as suggested above - *'See, Here, This'*- besides using this three-word expression, a briefer, and so better, is the use of the two-word phrase: 'Just walking' or 'Just breathing,' or 'I am.'

There is no need to set aside a regular time for this meditation. Meditation can, and should, take place at any time and in any place. Whenever there is no need for conventional, everyday A-mode of living, such as having a conversation with someone, the P-mode of meditation can be entered.

#

Only by being aware, by observation, will the mind disappear. There will be no control, for any control will be the ego acting. Gently, peacefully go about this; let it take its own time, it cannot be hurried. There is no you (your ego-self) present, so 'you' cannot be in control. Let it be like an autumn leaf gently falling and settling on the ground.

During this awareness, being in the present, thought itself will drop away. Thus the importance of choice-less awareness—to be without choice or opinion. The inner peaceful emptiness sees what is. During this state of choiceless awareness, there is neither *attraction* to, nor *aversion* from, any surrounding exterior or interior stimuli (sights, sounds, feelings, sensations, thoughts etc). As the mind focuses with present moment attention, gently and attentively on what is actually occurring within one's interior and exterior environments, there is a sense of deep calm and stillness.

When one becomes aware of one's awareness, one is in the present, choice-less mode of consciousness—the P-mode, the Awakened State. Here, by Grace, the breeze blows in through the open window; the knock at the door is answered.[66]

#

To be aware without choice, is to be truly aware—without any comment or judgment—of any thoughts and feelings. There is no reaction. In this way there is just watching. The mind is like a mirror—the image does not stick to it.

As has been said:
'The perfect man employs his mind as a mirror; it grasps nothing; it refuses nothing; it receives, but does not keep.'
 Chung-Tzu

This does not mean we become some kind of lifeless zombie. It is quite the contrary—everything becomes light and living and brings great joy. This *experiencing* brings us face-to-face with the truth.

#

When you realise that you are not aware or attentive, it is then that you are attentive! In the beginning one usually finds that having become aware, one seemingly immediately, re-enters the thinking—mentation—mode. It is important to know that there is no guilt in that you have become unaware. It will happen again and again—moving from the P-mode back into the A-mode—there has been no wrongdoing. Nearly all our education is based on mentation. It is good and useful for practically everything—except in the area of 'higher' consciousness, where it intrudes powerfully. But there is no point in making it into a problem; it is itself as much *That Which Is* as anything. Just calmly and simply return again to awareness. This precious time of awareness, the more one gets to know it, will become more and more frequent and natural.

Its essence—beauty and peace—will become missed in time when one finds oneself unnecessarily in the A-mode. One will, on realising that one is unaware, naturally without effort become aware; there will be no need for any mentation.

#

We cannot have a course of action laid down for us to follow. We are not given a direction here; where getting to x, y or z is the aim. The way is trackless. We do not need action here; what is needed is *present-experiencing* or *light*. 'Light' is a word which has many meanings but the one here is similar to that which is used in the expression 'shedding light on' something. More accurately, this refers to the light of consciousness. As in white water rafting, rather than fighting to maintain one's own objective *direction*, it is *guidance* that is needed in 'going with the flow'.

Above all we are called to "Wake Up!"

That is "Become aware."

When one wakens from the conventional A-mode to become aware in the P-mode, it is not a transition from one mode to another. Metaphorically it is not like transferring from one ship to another, different ship. Using the same metaphor, it is like getting out from under the dark undercover confines of a ship's lifeboat. (Traditionally, this has often been a favorite place for a ship's stow-a-way; 'veiled' by the lifeboat's cover.) Thus experiencing the freedom of being on board the large mother ship itself. The P-mode can be pictured as this being on board the ship itself; the A-mode being confined to the small lifeboat. This confinement represents the situation metaphorically when in the A-mode. This is an analogy that basic Pure Consciousness is always here; for even when one is in the A-mode, it is working in the background—but 'behind the veil' of the mind. It is covered by the veil of the habitual thinking-mode. There is no escape from this natural, given 'ground'. One can neither enter, nor leave this consciousness, because this is our basic consciousness. What happens when one 'wakes up' is that the A-mode of consciousness disappears, just as the darkness of a bedroom disappears when the curtains are opened on a bright morning. When we wake up, the 'light overcomes the darkness'. The darkening veil of thought is lifted and now there is the light of the present.

This light and its universality are mentioned in a Christian context:
'In him (the Word) was life, and that life was the light of men. The true light shines in the darkness and the darkness has not overcome it......The true light that gives light to every man was coming into the world.'[67]

#

Awareness means that whatever is happening in the moment is happening with total consciousness, so in awareness we are not standing impersonally aside from life. However, 'awareness' is neither personal nor impersonal. Awareness or attention is truly interested, and without judgement. It has no motive, no imaging, and uses no method.[68]

With a worrying, nagging problem—say, when one is immersed possibly in fear as to what will happen in the future—by 'waking up' and becoming aware, these worrying thoughts, or the problem behind them, will not miraculously disappear. However the problem will take on a different aspect. The problem will still be there; it is not ignored. But there will be a clearer mind that will deal with the problem. This will be because the brain's natural intelligence will be free to act. The problem will be seen in the inescapable present moment and will be treated more efficiently, and in proportional importance, than if tackled by the thoughts of the fearful, worrying ego.

This is because awareness does not come from the centre of ideas or reaction; this centre being the ego-self. Awareness comes from a much deeper centre. Thought produces theological beliefs whereas spiritual experience comes from a source other than thought.

#

Direct knowledge that we gain comes to us through two inborn mental powers. These are:

- The Direct knowledge that comes through the senses. This gives us knowledge only of things on the *outside*—on the physical plane.
- The Direct knowledge that comes through insight or intuition.   This enlightens us from a deeper—*inside*—level.

This matter of insight will be discussed further in the next chapter.

> > > > >

8 – INSIGHTFUL
REALISATION

The thrush, in Thomas Hardy's poem quoted in Chapter 2, seemed to express joy because of some 'blessed Hope, whereof he knew.' However, the passionless man was not aware of this, 'something joyous.' He represents those who do not accept that there can be anything, as it were, 'deeper.' They would insist, through careful reasoning, that truth can be arrived at by the use of reason only. The view is that one needs to rely purely and solely on the intellect. If this be so, the remainder of this study will be of no relevance. It will be only by seeking the truth through such fields as philosophy, theology, psychology, science or similar process, will any findings be worthy of consideration by them. So, this will be as far as they will go in this study. This is likely to be a materialist viewpoint (this will be discussed in Appendix C.)

However, this will not be the case for some who feel that just being aware, in itself, is not sufficient to satisfy the mystery of 'I AM'.

#

An answer to this was suggested in the last chapter, chapter 7. In this chapter the conditions that enable us to have a 'pure perception' of truth, the conditions for awareness, were discussed. The 'finger pointed' and the resulting action was handed over to the awakened, lone traveller. (Lone but not lonely—he or she can travel with many companions, known and unknown.) But this is by no means the whole story for (using the Christian metaphor of the Cross on which Jesus died) we have at this point only arrived at the central part of the cross —where the horizontal intersects with the vertical. At this point the inner is on the 'level' with the outer—that is on the periphery.

Using this metaphor of a cross—which can be used by any one of any belief or none, but having a deeper meaning to a Christian—the mental activity of reasoning can be imagined as being on the horizontal arm. Reasoning is an attempt to understand the essence of a thing by logical process, based either on evidence or an assumption taken as self-evident. Experiencing through reasoning can only remain on the 'thinking' level; experiencing cannot go deeper.

#

So, is it worthwhile to remain open; open to a deeper insight than exclusively meditating in the P-mode?

This study has considered a possible third mystery: the Beyond, because by not doing so would be ignoring a large part of the history of humanity. Before all this is thrown out, as many today in our mind-dominated society believe as being unworthy of consideration, we should have a care to take the warning of the 'bath water.' In chapter 3, early on at the beginning of the study, the warning was given:
'Note the following CAUTION: that in this study we should be careful not to throw the baby out with the bath water! We are warned that, when there is a loss of faith, and the 'old order' is thrown over, for whatever reason, there is much potential danger. '

This uses the metaphor of a poor family using the same water for bathing. After the family has bathed, in the usual pecking order, it needs care with what is done with the murky water left in the bath: make sure the baby is not thrown out unnoticed with it!

#

It was mentioned that through insight can come realisation— a 'dawning'—of a fact. In this case a very important fact can be realised from the insights gained through awareness. We see that the realisation of a fact, rather than believing a 'given' fact, is necessary.

Choosing, as an example, the topic of 'knowing who I am,' there follows some points, that can at first be anti-intuitive but need to be realised.

The conditions that enable us to have a 'pure perception' of truth, is when the mind is actively passive—as in a mirror the reflection is of only What Is. So whatever one is doing it is done with complete understanding. Such awareness results in a realisation that there is no separation between the knower and the known, the thinker and the thought, the observer of the rose and the rose itself. The mind and the experience are actually just one process: experiencing.
So when one 'sees', or realises, the fact that thought itself is 'me' and that it is thought that has created this complex being of 'me,' then the truth concerning the observer being the observed is seen. For when you and the rose are there, present together, thinking is not possible. There can be no ego-I present. There is just 'seeing'. There, both you and the flower are one. You and the flower, in deep presence, become one. When there is no thinking the observer becomes the observed. There is penetration one into the other; there is no longer a dualism, you are not two. There is only one. You are here and now; no thought can penetrate this intensity; only one can enter through the narrow gate of the present. At this point there is a new dimension which opens up—a non-

manifest dimension. This dimension is called *awareness*.

When it is seen, not intellectually but through insight, conflict ceases.

#

It was mentioned in chapter 5, that the *intuitive* part of the mind is a lot more powerful than we realise. It affects many of our decisions, '*but we are stuck with our inner intuitive stranger.*' The self is 'denied' by realising that it is not an actuality but exists only in the mind's reality—inside the head. However, it was said that an *insight* was needed together with a resulting *realisation* for this to become a reality to one. If it is realised not only through the *intellect* but through insight as a **fact**, that there is no *actual* 'ego-I' that I call myself, then the denial is brought about without effort or will-power.

We need to receive the gift of insight that me 'The Observer' is me 'The Observed'. No amount of intellectual theorising can bring about this realisation. But if you do try to, you will be using the intellect and the answer will be from the outer periphery of your ego-self. This will bring you to realise that, yes, you are a self but it cannot be *this particular* self, it must be some self which is other than your ego-I self.

The self is 'denied' by realising that our seeming ego-I is not an *actuality* but it is an ever-changing reality which virtually exists due to the mind's activity. This does need an *insight* with a resulting *realisation* for this to become a actuality to one.

#

Stating the truth is one thing,
realising it is another.

Realisation is an act of becoming fully aware of something as a fact.

#

One concept especially now has taken on an importance in this study: **insight**.   So it deserves a brief, but closer, look.

Chapter 7 ended with the statement that the direct knowledge that we gain comes to us through two inherent mental powers: (1) through the senses and (2) through insight or intuition. Both come directly. If truth is unknown, and if it cannot be answered from knowledge through the senses, then if it is to come at all it needs to come from the other source: through a perception of truth or insight. This enlightens us from a deeper—inside—level.

The discovery is made that the mind uses 'powers of the mind' other than that of mentation: mind activity. It is through these means that we may come to an even 'deeper' knowledge of the Truth—the 'Original Source'. They will have to come from sources different from that of thought.   In other words the mind will have received a perception which has 'bypassed'—as it were—the thinking process.

Dictionary definitions of these 'powers of the mind' - intuition as well as insight - are:

INSIGHT: the power of seeing into and understanding things; practical knowledge; enlightenment; a view into anything; awareness, often of one's own mental condition. (psych.)
Note that *insight* is defined in the dictionary not only as the power of seeing into and understanding things, but also as: enlightenment, awareness, often of one's own mental condition (or *psychological*); appreciation of the task or the puzzle.

INTUITION: the ability to understand something instinctively, without the need for conscious reasoning. This comes from the 'natural wisdom' of the brain.

#

Insight is a term seldom heard mentioned in Western Philosophy. In fact it tended generally to be ignored, or even denigrated, in the West. Insight can be thought to be *the seeing clearly of the essence of a thing.* This can often be either suddenly after disciplined meditation, or following a long struggle to understand something through reasoning.

Bertrand Russell, the great 20c philosopher, commented on insight, and mysticism in general, with a warning about it. He said the experience of insight is necessary to good creative work but it is not sufficient. The subjective certainty which it brings may be fatally misleading. The warning is that: 'An insight must be tested soberly when the divine intoxication has passed'.
He commented on the insight of a mystic which he says begins with the sense of a mystery unveiled, of a hidden wisdom now suddenly become certain beyond the possibility of a doubt. The sense of certainty and revelation comes earlier than any definite belief. The definite beliefs at which mystics arrive are the result of reflections upon the inarticulate experience gained in the moment of insight.

#

Philosophy itself has warnings sounded on it in this study; especially when connected with the Negative Approach to truth. However the middle road is important here: balancing thought with insight. There are these two branches of philosophical thinking: insight and reason. Above all insight can lead to a realisation of truth. There is a great deal of evidence that, possibly most, scientific discoveries have begun through an initial insight.

#

The source of truth is like the source of insight or intelligence—it is beyond what thought can grasp.

There seems to be a source of intelligence—some call it *Wisdom, Spirit, Contemplative Knowledge, Cosmic* or *supra-consciousness* and so on—which is processed by the brain but somehow 'bypasses' the thinking process.[69]

> ***Intelligence*** (here the meaning of which was referred to above) does not operate when the mind is in the A-Mode. Mentation has no part to play in the operation of this kind of intelligence. It operates when in the P-Mode. One thing intelligence discovers is what the mind is able to do and what it cannot do.

#

To obtain a fuller picture of insight, a brief look at the history of its use—and its neglect especially in Western Thought—will be useful.

As with many religions, Christianity was not *reasoned* into existence; it was founded originally on *insight*. Paul had a 'striking' revelation (insight) on his way to persecute Christians. Jesus (like Buddha) spent many days in the 'desert' before his ministry. He went on to teach his insight (inspiration) that the love of God and neighbour was more important than adherence to the laws proclaimed in the Jewish Old Testament.

Paul's New Testament message was that the Spirit gives life and that the word kills. Jesus, born a Jew, was inspired to proclaim the gift of the Spirit freeing mankind from having to adhere to restrictive laws.

Unfortunately, this 'Good News' has been ignored by many Christians ever since. They have ignored much of Jesus' teaching—that of the Love of God—and instead concentrated on the hard 'outer shell' which Jesus condemned—laws and the (dead) letter of the 'word'. Jesus knew the dangers of using words: the *word* which can cause much suffering. For example he said: "Do not suppose that I bring peace to the world, but a sword" (Matt10:34). The sword to which he referred is a spiritual weapon not a physical one. There is no evidence he was ever violent to another person and, indeed, he ordered Peter to put up his sword when Peter wished to physically defend Jesus from arrest (Matt 26:52-53). Also in Luke 12:51 he says: "Do you think I came to bring peace to the earth? No, I tell you but division." This seems strange coming from a man of peace. However Jesus must have known that his words —his positive-mode of teaching which he felt was necessary although putting himself in danger—would cause inevitable division. This is a good illustration of how using the positive approach—the A-mode—in order to 'tell the truth,' leads inevitably to division, fragmentation and distress.

#

The other branch of philosophical thinking—reason— plays a large part in this study, despite the cautions associated with 'thought' discussed throughout. So, of course, philosophy plays a large role in the 'inquiry of truth,' as Bacon was quoted as saying in the Preface.
The following are two examples of Western, pre-Christian, philosophical reasoning leading, through experience., to *insight* and the *realisation* of 'What Is' from the early years of the first millennium.

Plotinus (205-270AD) was a Greek philosopher, a Neo-Platonist, who suggested that we should manage without the use of reason. Reason, he said, cannot provide the evidence. "You can only apprehend the Infinite by a faculty that is superior to reason." And: "In this state of absorbed contemplation, there is no longer any question of holding an object in view; the vision is such that seeing and seen are one; object and act of vision have become identical." Plotinus himself experienced on a number of occasions a 'blissful union with the One.' "When the soul begins again to mount, it comes not to something foreign, but to its very self".

Marcus Aurelus, Roman Emperor and Stoic philosopher, said: 'Look within. Within is the fountain of the good, and it will ever bubble up, if thou wilt ever dig.' And: "Everything we hear is an opinion, not a fact. Everything we see is a perspective, not the truth."

#

The Roman emperor Constantine the Great, was the first Emperor to become a Christian. When he adopted Christianity as the Roman religion, he closed down philosophical thinking of any kind—both reasoning and insight.   As far as he did want to know the truth, he adopted belief in supernatural forces to do so by relying on —his description of the Bible as—inerrant 'divinely inspired' scriptures.   In other words, dependent on the knowledge derived from the written *words* of the Scriptures.

After long debates, the nature of Jesus and other problems were 'solved' using the intellects of theologians.   It was their solutions which had to be believed—full stop!   Those who agreed with the Church were called 'orthodox.'   Those who disagreed, such as the Gnostics, were called 'heretics.' Anything that was heretical was eliminated, as far as possible. Thus the Church had a secure hold on what was, and is, believed.

From the 12c onwards Scholastic reasoning appeared in the West, but this was controlled by the Roman Catholic Church. It had the supreme authority, and so, in the main, philosophy/ theology used thought and reasoning only.

However despite this persistent official use of mentation to try to come across truth, there has been throughout history groups of people like the Desert Fathers in the 3c, monks and nuns in monasteries, and by individuals, such as Meister Eckhart, St Theresa and John of the Cross who continued to use 'spiritual insight'. Thus, even in the West, *experiential* knowledge of 'That which permeates and organises the world' has been pursued throughout the ages.

In general, the Western World took the 'Positive Path' and the Eastern World the 'Negative Path' to truth. But the consequences of concentrating too much on one or the other approach—and not the middle path—can prove from experience to be unwise.

Coming to modern times, beginning in earnest some years after WWII, there became in the West a greater respect for and understanding of Eastern thought. It gradually became more widely known that insight is important in the study of truth—that is the 'Truth' which is referred to in this study. As mentioned, as insight had been neglected in the West, this could be called a revelation and has assisted in producing a *new life* outlook.

#

Truth is a part of 'that which is'. It is a *movement* or *act within that which is*. It actually *is*. Truth cannot be described, but it is an actuality which acts. Truth is not knowledge; it acts from moment to moment. The perception of Truth is an actual act— it is not truth *about* something.

#

After having an insight there should be an attempt to finalise it by describing it with words, to the best of our ability. By so doing we can use these statements to discuss or remind ourselves of it.

This insight has nothing to do with the intellect. If this is only *believed* to be true, then it is has no part to play in Truth—

except as a step towards it.

Thought can be used in the service of Truth—but only once the Truth has been realised inwardly.

Intuition, or insight, can bring us to a realisation, or a knowing, which has the ring of inner certainty.   This may not agree with a mind that has intellectual reasons to disagree.   This has caused us in the West to be very distrustful of it.   Usually we would rather trust in reason, our intellect.   Intuition is uncontrolled; flashes can come of true understanding or they may not.   Insights may be sought but they cannot be commanded.   This was illustrated above by suggesting that a window or door needs to be open for the 'wind to enter'; thus it can be considered as being a gift. Only by the constant use of testing each new *revelation*, in the light of reason and past experience, will the intuitive-power grow. However we do need to be aware of wishful thinking; for this also needs to be taken into consideration as a possible danger.

#

The following illustrates the two kinds of approach to Truth: one through the intellect, the other through insight.   It is concerned with 'opposites.'

Before this, 'opposites' will be considered briefly.   A thought, or a word, will always be connected with its opposite.   So, for instance, in actuality there is no such thing as 'good' alone. You cannot see 'good'—it exists only in the mind. And when you say that something is good it will immediately imply its opposite: that there is the possibility of bad. If there was no such thing as 'bad' then 'good' would not exist.

Shakespeare knew this when he wrote:

> 'There is nothing either good or bad,
> but thinking makes it so.'
>
> Hamlet. Act II Scene 2

Because thoughts are always dual, whatever the words used—

whether they are opinions, criticisms, beliefs, judgements or any other choice—there is always the potential of its opposite. Hence there is the need for *choice-less* awareness.

Jesus said: "Judge not". He added the dual consequence: "That you be not judged." He knew the contraries of actions as well as words.

#

Firstly, the intellectual approach.
Someone who used reason, the intellect, and who was interested in God and could be called a mystic, was Nicholas de Cusa. Nicholas, a mathematician, was born 1401. The concept of 'unity' was of great interest to him because he realised that Truth, God, was One and indivisible and was thus above and beyond Opposites. Truth itself could have no such thing as an opposite—it is One. Because Truth cannot have an opposite, opposites themselves needed to be considered also. Opposites are universal: the infinite and the finite, time and eternity, good and evil; the One and the Many; Unity and Diversity. and so on. The solution Nicholas arrived at, using metaphors, was his doctrine of the *'coincidence of opposites'.*

This was, briefly:
God is surrounded with a wall.
The wall's door is guarded by the proud spirit of Reason.
So this door has to be overcome if entry (to God) is ever to be gained.

That is:
God, or Truth, is surrounded with a (psychological) wall. This wall needs to be passed through in order to know God. But the only way through is by a door in the wall. The doorkeeper is the proud spirit of Reason, the intellect. Reason has to be overcome in order to pass through the wall. Reason says that it cannot be overcome except by a logical impossibility. An example of an impossibility would be for opposites both to happen at the

same time. For example, it is impossible logically for it to be early and late at the same time.   But Reason says: "The *coincidence of opposites* cannot logically be; you cannot have *before* at the same time as *after*. Therefore I proudly state that you cannot pass through this wall to know God." So the use of mentation must be overcome; thought must cease. The only way there can be the coincidence of opposites—where *before* is the same as *after*—is through the silencing of thought. This is the only possibility of being allowed passage through the door (to know God).

Nicholas therefore concludes it is only when opposites coincide —thought is dropped—that entry to God is possible.

This approach reflects the Western, mainly intellectual, initial approach which uses philosophy, theology and so on. He used reason to conclude that reason itself could not be the way of approach to God; and so ended by dismissing reason as a means of coming across Truth.

It follows that if on accepting this doctrine one thinks: 'I must not think. I must quieten the mind,' thought will still be continuing. This Positive approach will be like cleaning your muddy boots with a muddy cloth. The only course is to use the Negative Approach which, on the insightful realisation that there *is* this door in the wall through which one may pass, passes effortlessly through the door through *awareness*.

Secondly the insightful approach.

Concerning the principle of relativity and the identity of opposites, Chuang Tzu (370-287 BC) has been chosen here as a proponent for the negative, Eastern, viewpoint. Nicholas shared this same interest in 'opposites' as Chuang Tzu who lived about 1700 years before Nicholas and in a totally different society and environment. He arrived at a similar conclusion to de Cusa, but using this opposite—that is 'Negative'—approach.

His approach to these two relationships is that a wise person is not imprisoned by the ego-I; for his or her viewpoint is that of *both* 'I' *and* 'not-I' through direct intuition. Therefore, he sees both points of view: the rights and the wrongs on both sides of the argument. It has been said that Shakespeare had this ability and was thus able to construct his stories with the ability to understand both protagonists' views. He sees the right and wrongs of each side and so in the end both sides are portrayed with equal understanding and 'sympathy.'

This thing Chuang Tzu called 'the Pivot.' of the Tao[70]. The Pivot is the 'still' centre of the wheel. The Pivot of the Tao passes through the centre where all opposites meet. When a wise person centers on this Pivot, says Chuang, he or she is standing at the still centre of a wheel or circle, while the opposites of good and bad, yes and no, up and down chase each other around the circumference.

He said that if you do not consider 'right' without its mutual relationship 'wrong' then you do not understand a basic truth of the universe. It would be absurd to the talk about 'heaven' without that of 'earth'; 'negative' without 'positive.' The very axis of Tao is when objective and subjective are both without their opposites. And when all infinities converge at the centre through which the axis passes, negative and positive blend into an Infinite One.

Chuang Tzu's *'Pivot of the Tao'* and Nicholas' principle of the *'coincidence of opposites,'* despite being approached from very different viewpoints, reach a similar result.

#

Reference is made to what was quoted at the beginning of this study:
'It could be said of me that in this study I have only made up a bunch of other men's flowers, providing of my own the string

that ties them together.'

Running throughout history has been a consistent thread—
or string, which is insight—that ties together many voices
that have very similar messages.   With one voice, but
different languages, they speak over centuries from many,
very separate, cultures.

Besides Jesus, a very important person to discover, or rather
*un*cover, the way to Truth was the Buddha; born around 563
BCE.   There follows just two quotes from Buddhist writings
concerning their insight into the relationship between the
individual and Truth, and the understanding of our use of
'words' (discussed in 'Our Home Made World', Chapter 4):

> *1.   Indeed, the saving truth has never been preached
> by the Buddha, seeing that one has to realise it within
> oneself.*

> *2. Wishing to entice the blind, the Buddha playfully let
> words escape from his golden mouth; heaven and earth
> are filled ever since, with entangling briars.*

Another example of an insight from a very different time
(12th and 13th century) and place which was Germany:

> *Up then, noble soul! Put on thy jumping shoes which
> are 'intellect' and love, and overleap the worship of thy
> mental powers, overleap thine understanding and spring
> into the heart of God, into his hiddenness.*

NOTE: The word *'intellect'* is one of those words whose meaning
has changed over time. At the time Eckhart wrote the quotation

above, '*intellect*' had the meaning: '*immediate intuition*'. *Intellect*, then meant something totally distinct from *reason*. Reason, now, means enquiry and discourse (meaning the results of thought), whereas *intellect*, as used by Eckhart, means an *intimate penetration of truth*.

So Eckhart is saying: One must first use and then abandon the rationale and emotional path of 'word and discrimination' so that one may walk on the *intuitive path of realisation*.

#

The ego cannot through its own efforts come to this '*pearl of great price.*' Because this has nothing to do with 'my efforts' it can be thought of as a gift.

Paul believed that we couldn't force God to give us His Holy Spirit:

> *It is by grace that you have received this, without effort on your part.[71]*

Grace means being given a free gift, without it being earned.

Truth—*That Which Is*—is come across when we are in the P-mode of consciousness and is a result of an insight and realisation in the mind.
This is sometimes referred to as metaphysical[72] truth. (But what it is named doesn't matter.)

#

That Which Is seems to be simple and self-evident once you gain an insight into the actuality which is seen when directly experiencing in the P-mode. However because this deeply realised mystery cannot be named or described—except possibly in poetic terms—this must be stated in the necessary A-mode. This gives needed balance, for it will 'translate' this direct experiencing into religious explanations, or written into myths, poetry and so on. It does not mean that the P-mode of direct experiencing is bereft of joy, love, beauty and peace. It is quite the opposite! Realisation of the Truth brings joy and happiness.

Jesus said:

I have come that they may have life, and have it to the full. ^{John 10:10}

Paul said:

> But the fruit of the Spirit is love, joy, peace, patience, kindness, goodness, faithfulness, gentleness and self-control.

Gal: 5:22

#

However, if we are to know the Truth, these statements cannot be taken as tenets of a faith. They must not be intellectualised or taken to be *the* truth. This does not mean that they do not *point* to the Truth. Words can have an underlying truth to them.

#

The two commands of Jesus to 'love God' and to 'leave self behind' are both impossible for one who has not had the ego-self destroyed. Darkness can only be expelled by light, not by our efforts.

Whatever our true nature is—which cannot be known or observed by 'me-the-thinking-ego'—*seemingly* must partake itself of the nature of That Which Is. Whatever it is which realises this, which we cannot know, has no more need to realise itself than the sun needs light to light itself.

#

The more we try to achieve this realisation ourselves, the more subtle the ego is for returning through the back door.
Jesus said:

> 'Enter through the narrow gate. For wide is the gate and broad the road that leads to destruction. But small is the gate and narrow the road that leads to life, and only a few find it.'

Matt 7:13,14

It is only in another mode open to us that we can pass through this 'narrow gate'; the narrow gate which is *present-awareness* or *attention* which takes place in the P-mode of consciousness.

Again, darkness can only be expelled by light, not by our efforts.

As Paul said, quoting him again, we need to be awake:
> *Awake sleeper from the dead and*
> *Christ will shine upon you.*

#

The desire to achieve realisation involves some seeming paradoxes. One of these is: *That Which Observes* or *Sees* cannot be seen as an object or known by itself. It can be known only subjectively. When this seeing and knowing happens it must happen immediately. There can be no time interval between this seeing and knowing; for there is only experienc*ing*.

> 'You cannot see the seer of sight, you cannot hear the hearer of hearing, nor perceive the perceiver of perception, nor the knower of knowledge.'

The law of *reverse effect* is working here. For it is because we are searching for it, we lose it. We search because our mind does not see that it is trying to use *What Is* to seek *What Is*. The subject—of the desire to seek What Is—*IS* What Is. So the subject of the desire is the same as the object of the desire. There is nothing to be gained or to be sought after.

In Christian terms, this is your true self, your spirit, trying to obtain union with God, the Father, through God, the Holy Spirit.

However it is pointless for our true self to attempt to seek union with God, if the interpretation of Jesus' statements referred to in the statements below, is correct. Paul seems to say the same thing: *we are in that state now.*

Paul puts it this way:

God ... has seated us in the heavenly realms. [73]

Note Paul means that this is the **present** situation: we are **now** seated with God.

#

The ego, or self, cannot be who we really are. In fact, we cannot *say who* 'we' are in words.
Nevertheless, a Christian can read what Jesus said on the matter in John:
I am in the Father and the Father in me.
On that day you will realise that I am in the Father,
and you are in me, and I am in you.[74]

The Hindu would say:
'Thou Art That'.
In Sanskrit *'tat tvam asi'*: the immanent eternal Self, called the Atman, is one with the Absolute Principle of all existence, named Brahman.

#

Also mentioned before, our life is: a relationship with the world of things, a relationship with our fellow life forms and the relationships with our minds. But what is actually the relationship with our very 'selves' ? We know that our ego-self is an ever-changing, mind-produced entity, which is influenced from the past. So what self must there be to enable us to truly say: 'I am'? What is our most important relationship: our true self's relationship with the 'Ground of our Being'?

#

This Pure Observation, which seems not to be separate from the mind when in the P-mode, also seems to be something to do with the Universal, the Immeasurable, the Void—called by some 'God'. This must be associated with the 'Beyond,' which was referred to as the possible, third mystery mentioned in Chapter 2.

The subjective mind—the mind in the A-mode—therefore cannot make God an object of knowledge. The mystery must be inside.

Jesus was asked: "Who then can be saved?"
"What is impossible with men is possible with God".[75]

#

Again, it seems strange at first to realise that: on the one hand there is nothing that we are able to do, but on the other hand there is not the option to just say: 'O.K.' and then sit around doing nothing. We do act, but not independently. Although seemingly paradoxical, it could be called 'Dynamic Relaxation.' It is relaxed, in the sense that our egoless activity acts in harmony with nature—'going with the flow' means no effort when in the P-Mode of consciousness. It is not passive or static—it is relaxed but also dynamic. There is thus freedom—freedom from the exertion of ego-selfish needs, desires, ideas or theories which condition or draw boundaries.

Experiencing is only in the now; in the Eternal-Now. Making an effort to achieve some mind-produced aim means that we do not realise, through insight, that it is present here and now. We will not be 'In Tune With The Infinite'.

The Now can be the only time when we truly know who we are.

#

When we are asleep in our ego selfishness, we are unaware of the true Self.

When aware, with thoughts and other mind activities being observed without criticism, it becomes obvious that there is a ground or inmost centre of consciousness. It is That which always watches and witnesses the stream of experience whatever the outer circumstances. This is the pure consciousness of the true Self. This is the Self which accepts in this awareness the finite stream of experience consciously instead of unconsciously.

#

After realisation the process becomes conscious. One's state of mind and being at any moment will be able to be accepted without judgement. This is 'the love of yourself' as you must equally love your neighbour. You, in the P-mode, will accept consciously what you are, now.

#

There is no time interval in the seeing. This is not a solution that *takes time*. When time is involved it means that we are working towards a solution. It means that there is space between the observed and the observer.

It is possible that Jesus meant this when he said:

"If your eye be single, your whole body shall be full of light"

This is when the mind is in a state of passive 'negative' soil for the seed to flourish. In the *seeing* of this insight, there is the *doing* of it. It happens immediately. There is no mediation involved. This seems to be the truly religious mind: a mind that has no fear to face *that which is*—the truth. This mind can be thought of as a Faithful mind.

#

The freedom to accept the Now-experienc*ing* of the state of mind through mindfulness—and your emotional and physical state, as they are—is always the perfect and complete living in *this moment*. The ego-consciousness is essentially a complex of memories and anticipations; it is time-bound to the past and the future. The present moment does not, and cannot, exist to the ego. This can be seen when one dwells simply and solely on what is happening at this moment. For instance, when listening to and being aware of, simply and solely, one's breathing *at this moment*.

In this attended-moment one finds that memory, fear and anxiety vanish. Of course to look for these results will be our subtle ego looking!

#

Consciousness of this moment is pure, present attention. In this size-less point the ego cannot exist, as there is no 'space' between the observer and the observed.

The verse: 'The straight and narrow gate that leads to eternal life' could also be thought as referring—besides that suggested above—to *this moment*. So the 'narrow gate' can also be thought of as 'the present moment'.

By the paradox of non-duality* everything exists in Oneness in this infinitely small and timeless present moment. And, again paradoxically, this timeless moment is the Eternal Present.

(*Note re Non-duality. This basically means 'Not-two' and 'One undivided without a second'. Non-duality is the awareness of the One-ness of Spirit and that everything else is transitory and dependent on it. So non-duality means that any identification with common dualisms or opposites—such as conscious/unconscious, illusion/reality, male/female, living/dead, good/evil, particle/wave, one/not-one or one/many—means that the deeper actuality (of Being) is not understood. The duality, or separation *between the observer and the observed, is an illusion. One difficulty in understanding non-duality is that, actually, this cannot be named. By definition, once anything—even a philosophical or abstract idea—is named, paradoxically, immediately a duality has been created. To state that: "all things are one"* creates a distinction between "one" and "not-one"! Actually humanity—as well as everything else—is a non-fragmented wholeness at the deepest level of existence (the ground of Being). This duality, or separation between the observer and the observed, is an illusion which seems to have been discovered in Western science; more recently by way of quantum mechanics.)

Knowing who we are means we need have no worries about the future. This is where true security lies; it is in the 'inward' and never to be found in the 'outward'.

Jesus said:
> "*Do not be anxious for the morrow*" *Matt 6:34*

Repeating what Paul said above
> "*God ... has seated us in the heavenly real*ms."

#

This realisation of an eternal and inescapable present, or *Presence,* shifts our centre of consciousness. Our centre is no longer the dominating ego with its interminable thoughts needed to keep it alive.

#

We must be clear between who we actually are and who we (literally) *think* we are. If the difference between these two is not clear there will be a great danger of selfish individualism and antinomianism*.

(*Note re Antinomian: one who denies needing to obey the moral law: a person who believes that Christians are emancipated by the gospel from the obligation to keep the moral law; faith alone being the only thing necessary.)

We can see that we are trying to overcome our anxiety, boredom, anger, and fear by using that which is actually causing it—it being the mind. It is like trying, as has been described above but more graphically, to wiping blood off your hands with a blood-soaked cloth. There IS only anxiety, boredom, anger, and fear; no 'you' being anxious, bored, angry, or fearful.

#

You cannot leave this eternal dimension just as you cannot leave this moment. Realisation is not the creation of a new state of affairs but the bringing to consciousness of an eternal state which has always been there—our self, fully conscious; unlike our sleeping ego mind-world.

#

Realisation itself cannot be communicated by explanation or theory.
It has to be indicated with conceptual language such as using the mode of 'pointing': by telling stories, myths or parables.

After Jesus had told his disciples the Parable of the Seeds, previously referred to, they asked him why he spoke to the people in parables. He replied that the secrets of heaven have been given to them and not the people.

He goes on to give what seems to be another example of the *Law of Reverse Effect,* he says:
   Those who have will receive more and in abundance.
   But those who do not have will have taken from them, even
   what little they do have.
(However, see cautionary note below.)

But to answer the question directly he said:
   Through seeing they do not see;
   Through hearing they do not hear or understand
                    Matt 13: 11 and 13 This was also referred to by Paul above.
   <u>A cautionary note.</u>
The first of these two statements illustrates one of the problems

with communication (in the A-mode): that of misinterpreting the point that is being made. Nearly everything Jesus was teaching was to do with the 'inner'. His injunction to the centurion: 'Be content with your wages', was an exception and was referring to the outer!

And of course, the meaning must be realised by the individual him or herself.

Is this what we need each to do: 'Prepare the way for the Lord, make the rough places smooth for him?' Mark 1.3

#

By this natural unforced choice-less awareness, or mindfulness - when, in harmony with our minds' intellect, with thought silenced, and our heart-feelings, with energy - our hearts, minds and souls will allow the soil for the seed to flourish. In short this is the open door which will lead to Love. This could refer to the command which is first and foremost for a Christian:

> Love the Lord your God with all your heart, and
> with all your soul and with all your mind.
>
> Matt 22:34-40.

It is not possible to command a person to love something or someone. But what can happen, if there is no love to begin with, especially with an unmanifest Spirit, is for the development of a realisation that That, God, is the One who does the loving – with no conditions attached. An example of the very many, who have experienced this Love, is Dame, or Mother, Julian of Norwich. She wrote of her experiences through her revelations of the Crucified Christ. She wrote about these to convince her fellow citizens of the tremendous love Jesus Christ, God, had for each one of them. (This is briefly mentioned at the end of Appendix B, part 2) The realisation of being loved, undeservedly and unreservedly, and the immensity of the meaning of it, can result in that Love being returned. However weak this returned love, there will be no motive of gain for that person, other than a quest for intimate communion between them and God. In this returned true Love, there is no self – the self is left behind in this flame of love. Personal love is selfless; as can be experienced when two people merge in the communion of true love. In the same way, there is a self-merging in God through love. Whatever religion a mystic belongs to, whatever path they tread in Love, there is a question of self-mergence in Divinity. For instance, in Islam, which is the most transcendental of all the higher religions, Muslim mystics, called Sufis, see God as Absolute Love.

#

Jesus used 'pointing' in the Parable of the Seeds - Matt 13:3 – 9. The parable was of a farmer who sowed some seed: the birds ate that which fell on the path; some fell on rocky places where it took root but soon withered and some fell amongst thorns where it was choked. Some fell on good soil—the negative soil mentioned above—where it produced a good crop.
The context of this parable is the psychological or the spiritual understanding of truth.

#

This approach enables us to take an objective view of everyday life.
It is difficult to stop the flow of thoughts, imaginings and feelings which incessantly inhabit our minds. By simply paying attention to them without judgment, these become the objects seen by the mind: the observed and the observer being seen as one. By not giving them 'oxygen,' by ignoring them as clouds that drift by, they will fall away, as will any other object which is not identified with the self.

There will be insightful-knowing realisation of our true identity.

> > > > > >

9 – LIVING A NEW LIFE

Chapter 5 enquired into our knowing who we are: our true self. It was found that we have in fact two selves: one a transient, mind-produced self and the other, our true Self. In this final chapter of the study we take a further look at this Self.

Through the experiencing of the P-mode of consciousness we become aware—we wake up to the actuality of Being. We are aware of our self, acting in everyday life. It is to be accepted, not to be judged; held with esteem, but to be acknowledged for what it is. We know that the self that we are aware of is not our true self; it is not the true 'I' that 'I AM'. Self-awareness is like watching a film played out on a screen.

So, the question is this: If this self is not my true 'I,' what is it that is my true Self? Whatever it is, it is being differentiated on paper, in the A-mode, with a capital S: our true Self.

The mind, the intellect, will be able to ask the question but it will never be able to provide the true answer. This outer layer of consciousness is not the only layer. We are able to go 'deeper' as it were, to find the origin; to find that something which is uncaused within. For we experience one thing which has no cause; everything else, both within and without, has a cause. Observing/awareness/consciousness is not caused by anything; whatever happens this witnessing centre remains uncaused and unchanging.

#

In chapter 5 the question was asked: "So what is the nature of this Conscious Observer; the 'I AM' or 'That Which Is' which is aware, conscious?" By asking where this Observer is located, one will soon get to a point where it is realised that this place of observation cannot be known by the mind.

It is this Awareness of the awareness of self that is the source of the consciousness of the 'I' of 'I AM'. This Self-consciousness, or Awareness, is what was described as having no boundary; there is no limit to space within; it cannot be defined.

One's true Self, at one's inner centre, or core, is the true Observer. Observing at this moment. The Self is conscious of the self being aware, or consciously experiencing. This is Pure Consciousness; the very basis of our experiencing, our living.

The fact, which is seen with your eyes or heard with your ears or communicated through the mind – without the interference of thought but through the P-mode of consciousness - is the truth. It is this fundamental consciousness which is knowing the 'What Is' truth. It is not tarnished by any activity of the mind. One's true Self, at one's inner centre, will be that which is observing at this moment. And it can Observe the observer which was the awareness discussed in Chapter 7. It is at this point that 'me', the (homemade) observer, is the observed—by the Observer. The Observer, is aware of this observer.

It has been said of this Observer:
>   The eye cannot see it, but it is That by which the eye can see.
>   The ear cannot hear it, but it is That by which the ear can hear
>   The mind cannot think about it, but it is That by which the mind can think.

#

According to the findings of this study we cannot take any positive statements to be the truth. However, at this point it could be helpful to look at some positive statements made by others who have claimed to have discovered for themselves the truth of who their true Self is. There are of course many, many other positive statements attempting to give 'explanations' of the Primary Experiences by folk who have been blessed by them. What they say will obviously be positive statements. Keeping to the rules of this study, we have to acknowledge that when a statement is made which is positive, it is not the truth and we need to test for ourselves how close, or far, it is to pointing to the truth. A question is: Does their explanation have a possible 'ring of truth', based on our own primary experience, or maybe on just a good imagination, or even wishful thinking?

#

Keeping this *caution* in mind we can look briefly at what has been said about this Self, or centre of our being or consciousness—a centre which observes ceaselessly whether one is conscious of it or not.

It is claimed that by fulfilling certain conditions it is possible to go further, deeper inside, and find the centre, our true Self. Our Self can be associated with the divine Ground of our being. This Self is the opposite to the ego-self which is at the outer level, or on the periphery, of a person's psyche[76]. If you are willing to go deeper, it is said, it is possible to leave this outer periphery and—provided certain conditions are met—become aware deep down of another Self. Some have named this Self your *central core* or *soul*. This, according to those who experience it, is not just another self—it is, they say, your true Self.

It seems that in reaching this core one is said to be *centred* or *seated*—again as St. Paul said: We are (now) seated with

Christ, and that we are 'temples of the Holy Spirit', saying: 'Don't you know that you yourselves are God's temple and that God's Spirit lives in you?' [77]

In other words, in Christian terms, Christ Jesus enters our consciousness and there is a knowing relationship with the Spirit.[78]

'Here I am! I stand at the door and knock.'

#

As said, provided certain conditions are met, a person can come to a profound point where he or she can know their centre.

The following is a person arbitrarily chosen from all the countless men and women who have had this same, or fairly similar, experience: William Law (1686 - 1761). Law says that though God is present everywhere he is present to a person in the deepest and most central part of their soul. Our natural senses—the mind with its understanding, will and memory—cannot know God. Law says that it can only reach after him; but it cannot be the place in one where God lives. However, there is a root, or profundity, from which all these faculties, such as inherent mental and physical powers, proceed. They are like lines that come from a centre or branches from a tree. This depth Law calls the *centre*, *'fund'* or *bottom of the soul*. He states that this depth is the unity, the eternity, even the infinity of the soul—*infinity* for it is so infinite that nothing will satisfy it but the infinity of God.

Does this centre of our being hold this light which was in Jesus, of whom John says: 'This is the light that lights everyone who comes into the world?'[79]

The study has found, the 'modes of consciousness' often become the focus of attention. Consciousness is still a mystery to the scientist of today. We know that it is extremely important; there is nothing in the universe like consciousness.

Life would have no meaning without it; it is fundamentally essential. However, in this study we are not as interested in consciousness itself, as in its modes, its ways.

#

Another mystic Meister Eckhart (c1260 - c1328) says that:

'The more God is within, the more he is without.'

These notional facts—of God immanent and God transcendent —can be realised and experienced, if at all, only within the deepest part of one's soul—when one is *centred*. With God being both within and without, there is a position to be struck between introversion and extroversion—if one is to lead a balanced life. The temptation to one extreme or another is best avoided—neither to rush off to a monastery nor plunge into endless socialisation or hedonism.

As Shakespeare says in *Hamlet*, there are consequences:

Where joy most revels, grief doth most lament;
Grief joys, joy grieves, on slender accident.

This is another example of opposites: Joy and Grief are often close bed-fellows.

#

A person, who trusts only on the 'thinking A-mode' is likely to discount all this as nonsense, for: 'It cannot be proved logically or scientifically'. In this case he or she can be thought of as being on the periphery, or outer level of our consciousness—using A-mode surface-intelligence. He or she can be an aware, mindful 'observer;' but not willing to leave the periphery of thought; trusting in reason, logic, science. Appendix C will discuss this further. There is no criticism levelled at this person. For the state of being in the A-mode of consciousness is no less 'That

Which Is,' as being in the P-mode. This also follows a rule of the study—there is to be no judgement.

These deep, numinous inner experiences, are states partly governed, seemingly, by the temperament, together with the condition of their subjects.

Those who by Grace have these *inward* experiences, even if only dimly, will realise Truth in the P-mode. But they will express them, as mentioned, in differing words and in many varieties of ways depending on their spiritual and religious contexts. *Outwardly*, at the A-mode level, Truth remains a mystery as it cannot be told or described. However, surely this cannot be a cause of regret. For without some mystery, or without some experiences to make one marvel, our lives would be so much the poorer.

#

This study was begun by a believing Christian putting aside, temporarily, what was believed to be the truth. True seekers (whatever their beliefs) are prepared to examine all preconceptions. If limits are placed, knowingly or unconsciously, upon the pursuit of truth then truth itself is the casualty. *Faith* is the honest pursuit of truth wherever it leads.

Having tried to understand writings of many who claim to have come across truth—both in the Eastern and the Western traditions—it remains to reflect on these; while remaining aware of the rules set down for the study.

#

In having an open mind to enquire into truth, there has been revealed a hidden world or dimension.

#

The results of this study have led to the feeling of freedom and consequently, that one is living a different—in fact a NEW—

life.

'New' is used in two ways.

#

When in the P-mode one is 'awake,' aware; one experiences each moment as being new.

In these moments one comes to see and feel the 'given world' as it is, **is**; and not as it is named. This very simple "opening of the eyes" brings about the most wonderful change of understanding and living, and shows that many of our most baffling problems are virtual. This may sound like an oversimplification because most people imagine themselves to be fully enough aware of the present already. But, through experiencing awareness, we see that this is far from true.

This seems similar to what Peter described as being: "called out of darkness into his wonderful light." The old life lived in darkness is transformed into a new life of light.

We know, through insightful realisation and through meditation, that our inside and outside truly exist together in this dimension—in this ground: a ground of Being which has no definition. But it may be suggested that it can be named 'God'. (Any name will do of course; illustrated by the fact that there are as many names for it as there are religions.)

A person, who has experienced being aware of whatever is being experienced, however briefly, through insightful realisation, will know that this is a fundamentally new dimension. A dimension in which one is experiencing a new quality, a new feeling, of life.

When living the 'old' ego-centric life, perhaps with the 'lifting of the veil' or the 'opening of a door,' the P-mode of awareness happens. The 'Beyond' mystery of new life is experienced; it happens immediately; for it cannot be 'worked towards.' It is that one's world is conscious of two centres: that of being *ego*-centred and that of being, what we can now described as, *God*-centred. Even if it is subconscious, the tension between our two selves is released.   In everyday life, when the P-mode occurs, meditation takes place; with one's true centre experiencing the cinematic story being played out on the screen *A*-mode of consciousness.

#

Nicholas de Cusa wrestled with the problem, that one could not enter through the 'wall that separated us from God,' by the power of reason. By becoming 'unreasonably illogical' (in the psychological sense) in the P-mode, there is the joy and freedom in knowing that we are all fundamentally One. My Being is your Being – Both /And. Your 'I' is my 'I'. All 'I's are the same One **I**; One consciousness, One Self, One 'I Am.'

#

There is no possible means by which we can analyse That Which Is – which now may be named *God* - in order to describe Him/Her/It. But we do know that this ground in which we exist is not just a blind force. For we—who are ourselves conscious—are embraced by and are part of this non-fragmented Oneness. Thus, in this, there are indefinable feelings of intimacy.

Now here is the thing: this *'indefinable feeling of intimacy.'*

'Love' has been mentioned a number of times. All things have their opposites except two qualities of being: Love and Beauty. Both are fundamental; neither can be materialised by the mind. Love simply IS. It cannot be conjured up by the mind. It is when in the P-mode of consciousness that one may experience this something behind the 'screen.' This has the feeling of light and warmth which one can only be described as Love.

#

This *Beyond* need no longer be termed in this way now. It is no longer a far away *beyond* but to the contrary: It—God—is in fact closer to us than our hands and feet. Rather than being 'beyond' us, God is closer than we are to ourselves. It is as Jesus stated: we are in Him and He is in us—his Spirit is with us. Each individual, of course, will translate this concept/wording in their own personal way. This is because the coming across of Truth is uniquely personal for everyone.

God is apprehended or perceived when the mind is in the wordless P-mode of consciousness. No longer can one try to rely entirely on the intellect, but one can walk on trustingly, through Faith, in God's Spirit—which Paul describes as giving life.

This gives a freedom and a feeling of newness of life. This freedom is not a freedom *from* but a state *of* mind. One can trustingly, rationally, 'go with the flow'. We are *here* and *now* and, in fact, there is nothing we can do about this. Everything is *as it is*; which can mean that the present is perfect.

No longer is the viewpoint of life seen from an ego-centre. The A-mode's command to love God is no longer relevant. The love of God does not need to be ordered; indeed, Love cannot be commanded. This new life now revolves around God as the centre. A saying referring to this is: *'Let go and let God.'*

It is important to be reminded of the warning that if you are desiring to achieve this or to gain it for oneself, then the freely given Grace of God will be hindered by one's own ego-desires, with their never-satisfied need for self-aggrandisement.

#

The second reason for entitling this chapter: *new* life is that *New* can be used in the sense that it is *forever* new. It is being *renewed* moment by moment. This word 'new' is not being used in the sense that a thing that is now new will in time become old, the opposite to new. This is because every moment **is** new and therefore it is living; it is shed of the past. There is no past. Jesus said: "Leave the dead to bury the dead."[80]

#

Meditation is like moving out of darkness into a marvelous light.[81] It has nothing to do with intellect. It leads to insight and intuition.[82] It also gives a sense of living in a great space; there is a sense of the unity of all things.

One of Jesus' parables was about the soil. A seed can fall into poor or good soil. This silence of the mind is like fertile soil into which the alternatives are placed. If the seed is planted with energy it will mature. Listening, or awareness, is analogous to the soil. This listening is done with the attention, described as being choice-less; there is no intellectual interference of judging or evaluating; it is without choice and so the ego does not corrupt the experiencing.

Above all we must be awake and be aware. We will keep falling asleep—keep finding ourselves in the world of the mind, unconscious, dreaming. Directly we do find that we are asleep, all we need to do—all we can do—is to just: Wake up!

One can move (psychologically) effortlessly in the world—as defined elsewhere—but not be part of the world. We can live in the world but the world need not live in us.

We can walk now seamlessly in both of our two worlds. Living in the actual, given world 'supports,' and is basic to our life in the real, conventional world. For through meditation, we will be centred in our Self, in the here and now. There will be a knowing-awareness of our self, with its activities, as we live in the world of thought.
In this way the brain and mind - however mysterious the brain/mind relationship - will work together in harmony.

Our two worlds, lived together, will be in the fullness of an ever new life.

#

Meditation is the movement of Love. Unlike the result of drugs, the mind can enter into itself and plunge deeper and deeper—along the vertical of the cross, so to speak—until all measurement ceases.

Here, when at the centre - this still place - there is love, peace, order and beauty.

God here is known in our subjective life; being the source and ground of our BEING.

#

Of our three elements, it is the body and psyche which are the observed. Our third component part, our Spirit, is our essential being. It is that which observes, and by which we experience and which exists at our centre. It is the constant 'I AM' which is always there/here, behind all our outer and inner experiences. But It, Itself, the Beyond, cannot be discovered in, or through, our experiences. The Beyond, or Spirit, is BEING.

#

So, referring to the point made earlier: there is a further very important factor to be aware of. Besides the basic mode of consciousness—the awareness of our body, mind, feelings and so on—there must also be the awareness of this Self—our true Self at the ground of our Being.

Life is lived in a new way when you are centred; that is when one is *present*. Here, whatever the circumstances, one can be conscious that one **IS**.

At our centre is That Which Is; That Which Knows. It cannot be made an object. By turning inwards away from the objective outer, we may reach this depth, which, William Law calls the *centre,* '*fund*' or *bottom of the soul.* He claims that God is present everywhere, yet he is present to a person in the deepest and most central part of their soul.   The mind, with its understanding, will and memory, cannot *know* God. Law says that it can only *reach* after him.

#

And now, the last few lines from Emerson's poem, which refers to the rose growing outside his window, being perfect in all of its living stages. The poem then concludes with reference to humanity:

But man postpones or remembers;

he does not live in the present,
but with reverted eye laments the past,
or, heedless of the riches that surround him,
he stands on tiptoe to foresee the future.

He cannot be happy and strong
until he too lies with nature
in the present, above time.

Ralph Waldo Emerson (1803 to 1882)

#

When applied to life it is the journey that matters not the destination. It is in thinking about arriving that induces tiredness to the journey. When life's purpose is separate from the living of it—by the intellect—frustrations arise. Just as Love has no other purpose apart from loving, so life has no other purpose than to live. It has its own purpose. Questions like: 'Why are we here?' do not arise. That is, *psychologically* they do not arise.   However, they can be intellectually stimulating! To think of a point of arrival is to produce a static state. Just as Love has no purpose other than loving, so it is for life. One does not arrive at a spiritual goal. Life, if it is to be life, is dynamic and so life's purpose is achieved when it is

dynamically acted in the Now. The NOW: THAT is the point of life.
Life has no destination; it is constantly flowing.

Life can prove frustrating and painful if it is lived totally in the A-mode of consciousness. One is constrained by such things as religious laws (which by the way will have been thought up by someone) and one is thinking of the past and the future much of the time. The aim of life is discovered in the living of it. Every point on the journey of life has within it its aim and purpose. Because of this fact, one can depart at any point on the life-journey and, although with much grief no doubt, have no regrets that its aim or purpose has not been achieved. Fulfilment is from one moment to the next; in the Ever-New, Eternal Present.

#

Despite the seeming counter-intuitiveness of it, it is in the insight that we are **all one** that there is true security.

The Universe is whole. It is *non-dual.* It, Being, is actually undivided. All are secure within it. Many religions have this at their heart: God or Being, or whatever name is given to It, holds them in unity and security at this centre; a centre which has no periphery.

#

Paradoxically, despite this unity, it is the individual human being who has the ultimate responsibility. For only he or she—that is *each one of us alone*—can know the Truth for ourselves.

In his book '*The Undiscovered Self*' Jung wrote:

… happiness and contentment, equability of soul and meaningfulness of life—these can be experienced only by the individual and not by the State. I am … concerned with the fate of the individual human being: that infinitesimal unit on whom a world depends, and in whom, if we read the meaning of the Christian message aright, even God seeks his goal.

#

It is through the experiencing of the relationships we have in our everyday, ordinary life - with our fellow humans, nature and our inner thoughts - that we can see ourselves as we are. Life continues as one has always lived it. Again, nothing need be changed, neither life nor beliefs. However, this study may possibly have an effect on these; even to the extent that one feels the freedom of a 'new' life. The ego-self is seen; the individual natural surface-self does not disappear in some puff of smoke. However, the feeling of '*I AM*' will not be corrupted by '*I (my ego-self) am at the centre of the universe.*' We have to say that: 'I'—my true Self or soul or whatever name one wishes to use—with the observer being the observed, is no longer an **enigma**. We no longer have to think who we are, we know who we are. Also, we know through insight that if our eyes are not blinded or deceived by the mind—just pure consciousness in the P-mode as if they are just a mirror—then we find that there is actually no **riddle** of life to be solved.
To the mind the Way of Life is a riddle similar to the Crucifixion: 'To the Jews [the moralists] a stumbling block and to the Greeks [the logicians] foolishness.' 1Cor 1:23
        This verse will be referred to more fully in Appendix C.

But to awareness, with no-mind influence, this life in the P-mode will be the 'Life beyond Seeking.'

#

When we are in the P-mode we are conscious of That Which Is: the boundless, All-Loving 'I Am.' We find that the **mystery** of the Beyond, which is inside that which was once an enigma, is no longer a problem to be solved. This is a mystery which remains untold but is a mystery which is to be lived, experienced and enjoyed with courage.

Life may indeed be thought a **riddle**, wrapped in a **mystery**, inside an **enigma**. Only from the inside of this **enigma**, which is this Self, can the **mystery**, which we call 'God,' the Beyond, and in which the **riddle** of life resides, be solved.

What a privilege to have this opportunity and what a disaster if we do not take it; at least be open to it, whatever background we have.

#

The study suggests that we all need to be
living *New Lives*.

THIS IS IT!

****

PART THREE - WALKING ON!

10 - AFTERWORD

❖ ❖ ❖

Literally an hour before I planned to sit down and write this chapter, I came across the following. The passage is from an interview with a famous and much loved actor. In the article he was asked why he made a podcast series, entitled *questions of Faith*. His answer was that as a Christian, he felt it incumbent on himself to understand the other two Abrahamic faiths, Judaism and Islam. He said that he was troubled looking at the world and seeing such division and friction. He wanted to see if there is anything that can be done to bring people together.

#

This study, which was begun partly because of such 'religious' questions, has concluded that learning about and trying to understand one another's faiths, commendable as this is, will not solve the problem. This is because thought activity is the cause of the problem and can, at best, only paper over the cracks. The better course is, instead of analysing the *differences*, that we concentrate on what is *common*. It was this desire to see how we can come across truth in this way that two polar opposites were chosen: contrasting seemingly irreconcilable differences between the positive and negative approaches to truth. Throughout the study by looking at the comparisons between them concerning certain corresponding important issues or topics, it was seen (*seen* that is in *my* opinion; for it is important that every individual needs to come to his or her own insightful realisation) that they could be reconciled. However, if we are at the A-mode level of consciousness, with its mentation and with the centre being the ego-I, there always will be much room for argument and differing opinions over some, or all, of these comparisons. But the study set out to prevent, as far as possible, argument taking place. It was found that the mode of consciousness in which argument takes place, in the A-mode, is a dimension in which truth cannot be come across. By forming a synthesis between these approaches, it was found that from the two opposites (as with heads and tails of a coin) a 'higher' third (the valuable coin itself, to complete the metaphor) has appeared: a middle Way.

#

The enquiry into the three mysteries introduced in Chapter 2 led to the consideration of the mystery of the 'Beyond' which was associated with our 'inside' enigma. But, in order to do this, the first of the three mysteries required the solution to the enigma: Who is it that can say: "I am"? This needed a psychological approach.

After Chapter 7, the Way was able to look at the mystery of the Beyond. Thus, the approach changed from being psychological to a 'spiritual' one, using insightful realisation.
So, the enquiry ended with there being both negative and positive findings.

#

Firstly, the negative approach.

> (1) <u>Negatively</u>: it is not my ego-self.
> 'I am not this, I am not that.' Or the Hindu 'neti, neti'

The study began with a look at 'thought' - at its obvious benefits and its many drawbacks. It is a world of relativity; the world of manifest phenomena, the world where everything has its opposite. Our conventional life is lived in, what I named, the A-mode of consciousness. It is a world of duality, where we and everything are all separate. It is a world ruled by conceptual thinking. It sees one thing at a time. It was named our 'homemade world.' This is the world – seemingly, the one of two he mentions - that Jesus claimed he had overcome: 'In me you will have peace. In this world you will have trouble. But take heart! I have overcome the world.' (John 16:33) It is a world dominated by the conceptual area of our brains – the interpreter or story-maker. In this area such things as language, recognition, and characterisation are made. This is recognised by many as being mainly associated with the left side of the brain. These functions are felt to lead to the absolute conviction of a sensation of a self: I am.

Chapter 6, discussed the two worlds we live in, the Homemade and the Given. The former being the world of duality. At the end of the next chapter, Chapter 7, we arrived at non-duality; reached through meditation and the P-mode of consciousness. This is more to do with the parts of the brain which work by finding meaning, understanding and perceiving the whole picture; being creative, processing space and experiencing emotion. So, the study changed at the end of Chapter 7. There it was noted that Direct knowledge comes from two sources: through the senses and through insight or intuition. Accordingly, the study moved to considering non-conceptual insight. In this mode the world can be seen as one unified whole.

This has been named non-duality and can be loosely described as using the Eastern negative approach: the experiential truth—That Which Is. We can also say now: 'This Which Is.'[83] This is the world that Jesus said that God so loved.

#

Many make further progress in knowing the *Way* of IT, by entering further within, using awareness and mindfulness: the medium of meditation and also the use of Intelligence. One can follow, or 'live,' the Way; but it cannot be described.

IT is THAT Which IS, which is No-thing. IT is measureless, formless and timeless. This mystery of the Source, referred to as 'God,' is limited neither by space or time. IT is infinite consciousness and each one of us, as undivided one, has the same point of view as IT.

As the Hindu says: 'Thou art That ' (tat, tvam, asi).
As Meister Eckhart wrote:

> 'The eye through which I see God is the same eye through which God sees me; my eye and God's eye are one eye, one seeing, one knowing, one love.'

Until relatively recently, Western commentators, in their more limited understanding of Eastern thought, often called it *nihilistic*[84]. More recently, although such words as *no-thing* seem to have a negative connotation, their meaning can be seen to point to quite the opposite. Eckhart's comment, using the same mystical insights, illustrates this difficulty.

#

Secondly, the positive approach.
(2) Positively; in the A-mode.

In this study, it was found that using the positive A-mode alone cannot lead to Truth. However, it is no enemy; indeed, it is a valuable ally along the path to Truth. It often leads, as in the study, to being the finger that points to the uncovering of the fact which is finally achieved through the negative, P-mode, approach. Thus, the positive use of the thinking, intelligent mind, often plays a major, important part in the path to Truth.

In order to put forward reasonable, intelligent, positive answers, we do need to use theology and philosophy; science and religion. In doing so, we must remember the nature and danger of using mentation in order to discuss theological and philosophical topics.

#

To contrast this negative approach, Appendix C is attached; so as to illustrate the Positive approaches to Truth. These two traditional ways, used by the West, are theology and science.

#

A question put at the study's beginning was: *If the Truth be known, would it bring cessation of war*? – the madness of which was conveyed in the two short poems by Thomas Hardy. Today with many in society unconscious of the Untold Truth —with continuing competition between individuals, nations, races, belief-religions and so on—Truth remains hidden within homemade worlds. It is those who live in time, who are living in the A-mode of consciousness, it is they who do the persecuting and make the wars. They either venerate the past, using traditional, conservative memory, or trust in the future: the utopian future dream.
On the other hand, it can be seen that people who are the peace makers will be those whose main world views lie outside time, and have the insight that the world is one whole.

As mentioned at the end of Part 1: When we see that the behavior of humanity cannot be changed by using thought alone—nor by attempting to impose a solution from the outside—we will find that truth will lead us to realise that change can only take place from within; that is on the inside. That is why the only person you can change is yourself.

Only when we can enter the dimension of the 'given world,' balancing our 'home-made world,' will we find peace—for the individual first and then, as it consists only of individuals, society.

#

Standing on the shoulders of people who through thousands of years have sought after truth, I knew that I was 'reinventing the wheel.' But there was a need to understand this particular 'wheel' for myself—as it has to be so 'insightfully realised' by every individual.

At this now-point in life, and with every succeeding point, in knowing the truth, life may now be lived in freedom. As Jesus said (John 8:32):

'You shall know the truth and the truth shall make you free.'

So, in actuality, by sacrificing everything - in Christian terms: 'we are crucified with Christ' - we are now free to live fully in our everyday, conventional world; acting out our story on the stage of life by joining in the dance; finding pleasure in the playing of our parts on its stage with our fellow actors - travellers on the Way - with courage, love and compassion.

When during our travels we are open and aware, through meditation, or in the brief moment between two thoughts, we become silent, we are reduced to simply listening to 'What Is' - now. Unintentional thoughts are listened to, without comment or judgement, as one would the sound of rain. Here everything is as it is – infinite.   From the ever-present background, will come the faith that God is actual, and need not be sought in any particular direction, or conceived in any particular way.

Here we will know the consciousness and bliss of knowing that highest form of meaningful relationship:

that between God and Mankind, which is Love.

#

So, in the awareness of the P-mode:
> *Listen to the rain on the window.*

And in the awareness of the A-mode:
> *Hear the words: '**I am** with you always.'*

At this point finally, using the words of Shakespeare's Hamlet:

"The rest is silence"!

****

APPENDICES

APPENDIX A - BIBLIOGRAPHY

AUTHOR	TITLE	PUBLISHER	DATE
Bohm D	Thought as a System	Routledge	1992
Bohm D	Wholeness and the Implicate Order	Routledge	1980
Campbell J	Grammatical Man	Simon & Shuster	1982
Chuang Tzu	The Book of Chuang Tzu	Penguin Classics	2006
Fox A	Dean Inge	Murray	1960
Happold F.C.	Mysticism - A Study and Anthology	Pelican	1963
Hofstadter & Dennet	The Mind's I	Penguin	1981
Huxley A	The Perennial Philosophy	Fontana	1946
Inge W.R.	Mysticism in Religion	Hutchinson's U.P	1948
Krishnamurti J	First and Last Freedom	Gollancz	1954

Krishnamurti J	The Awakening of Intelligence	Harper	1973
Krishnamurti Ed. M.Lutyens	Freedom from the Known	HarperCollins	1969
Krishnamurti Ed. M.Lutyens	The Only Revolution	Gollancz	1973
Krishnamurti J + Bohm D	The Ending of Time	Harper	1985
Merton T	The Way of Chuang Tzu	New Directions	1965
Osho	Hsin Hsin Ming	Osho Media	2013
Panikkar R	The Rhythm of Being	Orbis	2010
Thatcher C	Just Seeing	Buddhist P.S.	2011
Underhill E	Mysticism	Methuen	1911
Watts, Alan	The Book	Vintage	1989
Watts, Alan	The Way of Zen	Pelican	1957
Watts, Alan	Behold the Spirit	Random House	1947
Zaehner R.C	Mysticism - Sacred and Profane	Oxford Paperbacks	1961

APPENDIX B -
THE GRACE

INTRODUCTION

This section is a copy of a series of three articles which were written for and published in a church magazine. This was in answer to the editor who had asked for contributions to the magazine.

I chose, as a vehicle for discussion, the Christian prayer called 'The Grace'. This was in order to promote discussion as to how the 'negative' approach (a term not used in the articles) could be used to look positively at some tenets of the Christian message.

For many years and with many vicars I have tried to ask why they do not take a fresh look at the Church's theology.

The Creeds were formed by the early Christians, who had Jewish backgrounds, assisted eventually by the power of the first Christian Roman Emperor. So much has been learned in the meantime that some movement within the Creeds would seem to be vital if the Gospel is to flourish.

Jesus' preached that God was a God of love:
'The Law came from Moses, grace and truth
came through Jesus Christ.'[85]

The Old Law was superseded by the New Law of Love. His title for God being 'Father, Abba.'

Let us seek the truth as best we can, but let us think carefully when using the word 'that kills.'

****

THE GRACE - 1

Some Thoughts (1)

The Grace of our Lord Jesus Christ, And the Love of God,
And the Fellowship of the Holy Spirit,
Be with us all, ever more.

The Grace is a prayer with which we often end a fellowship meeting. The custom at St X's is that many do this with our eyes open; communicating visually with the others in the group.

What if an enquirer was to ask you to explain what was behind this prayer, how would you answer? The best response for me would be to arrange for them an interview with the vicar! But what explanation would you give?[86]

Maybe then a sharing of some random, personal thoughts and questions on this prayer may be of some value, and better still may provoke others, much more capable and worthy, into making further comment.
#

The Grace naturally divides up into three parts. It is sensible to consider each part in the order that they appear.

…………..

Firstly, then:
'The Grace of our Lord Jesus Christ'

To one who knew him in his humanity, Jesus was a man 'full of grace and truth' [87] Luke says of his childhood: 'The child grew and became strong; he was filled with wisdom, and the grace of God was upon him.'[88] John continues: 'From the fullness of his grace we have all received one blessing after another. For the law was given by Moses; grace and truth came through Jesus Christ.[89]

The word 'grace' is variously defined in the dictionary. It is used in many ways: there is natural, animal grace, and there is human grace, and there is 'spiritual' grace. It is this last mentioned grace which we consider here. The best way to get the gist of a 'spiritual' word such as grace is by looking at some examples of its use. One example is Paul's use of 'grace' in the openings of some of his letters: 'grace and peace (be given) to you from God our Father and the Lord Jesus Christ'.[90] He often closes his letters also with the prayer for 'the grace of our Lord Jesus'[91] Another example is the acknowledgement of 'the grace of God *given'*. This can be seen in Paul's admission that he was changed from being a persecutor to a defender of the Gospel: 'But by the grace of God I am what I am, and his grace to me was not without effect,'[92]

Grace is a word not much heard today; although it is a lovely traditional name, Grace is not now, as far as I know, a popular baptismal girl's name. Many people seemingly do not experience the 'Grace of our Lord Jesus Christ' today. Why is this? And if we do not experience it, how can we come to do so?

One reason for the 'why?' seems to be the kind of society we now live in. The two main characteristics of our society today are noise and speed. It has become a technologically, mind-centred world, divorced a long way from Nature. The answer to the 'how?' is, of course, we can ourselves do nothing positive. We can do nothing ourselves to gain the grace of Jesus and—which is the same—the grace of God. Paul, earlier in the verse quoted above, puts his finger on it by saying: ' ... his grace to me was not without effect. No, I worked harder than all of them - yet *not I*, but the grace of God that was with me.' The New Testament claims that this 'grace of God' became known and was experienced through Jesus. Jesus makes us aware of God's grace through his grace. This was one of the things Jesus referred to when he said: 'Anyone who has seen me has seen the Father' [93].

Notice that we pray for the grace of our *Lord Jesus Christ* and not *Christ Jesus*. I take the change in position of the two names *Jesus Christ* and *Christ Jesus*, often in Paul's writings, to usually mean: Jesus in his humanity before his death and Jesus in his risen life after his death, respectively. If this is so then we are praying for the grace that Jesus, when in his humanity, showed to all. This same grace operates today. We can do nothing positive to earn or merit God's grace[94] This is indeed a blow to our pride, for my 'me' wants to be able to claim some credit so that I can say: "Here in the grace of God I stand". In fact, my 'me', my self or ego, or whatever one wants to call it, has to be 'left behind', 'denied', 'lost'[95]

God's grace can be thought of as an unmerited gift from God and together with it - and this is a test that the grace of the Lord is with us - will come peace.

We know we can do nothing of worth without this grace. So we ourselves need to do nothing—especially not by using thought or worry,[96] nor by judging[97], especially ourselves, nor by the effort of disciplining ourselves and becoming different to what we are now—as the hymn says: 'Just as I am without one plea ....'. For all self-effort to become someone different only reinforces my 'me'. God accepts us as we are, *now*: as the hymn says: ' .. but that thy blood was shed for me'. So does God withhold his gift for any reason? Knowing that God is Love, we cannot suppose so. We realise that we do run the risk of *presumption* by saying this. However we must surely come to the realisation that, unworthy as we are, His grace must always be here; just as Paul experienced:[98] Just so, his Risen presence is always with us.[99] If we realise this, not just intellectually, not just verbally as in reciting a creed, but really passionately realise it in our hearts, we will be, figuratively, opening the door. We cannot command or coerce the Lord to give us his grace and truth, but he said that he 'stood at our door' [100] It is like opening a window to allow the breeze to enter the room: we 'open the door'. This is a negative thing. For by the action we take we do not directly cause the thing to happen. We negatively remove the blockages that prevent us from an awareness of, and thus to experience in our life, the gift of the grace of God and of His Son Jesus Christ. It is this that is a supremely positive thing. So the negative approach allows a very positive thing to possibly happen.

The New Testament sees this as awakening 'from darkness into his wonderful light' [101] The darkness is the darkness of 'spiritual' death in which we live when we are dominated by our minds, with our ever-circling thoughts around the centre that we call 'self'. We don't have to search for light, we naturally open our eyes to see it. There will be light when we remove the barriers of darkness that create the darkness.

So, with the grace of our Lord Jesus Christ we can respond to the Ephesians' wake-up call 'that we too may live a new life'[102] - every day:

**Wake up, O sleeper,
rise from the dead, and
Christ will shine on you.** [18]

> > > > >

THE GRACE - 2

Some Thoughts (2)

The Grace of our Lord Jesus Christ, **And the Love of God,**
And the Fellowship of the Holy Spirit,
Be with us all, ever more.

In the second part of The Grace we pray that *'the Love of God'* be
with us all'. What would one say to a non-Christian of today who
wishes to know what is behind such a statement? Here are some
thoughts and questions, among an infinity, that could be said.
What would yours be?

#

It is an impossibility to describe, in words, the meaning of the
term 'the Love of God'. The best approach to the understanding
and knowledge of 'the Love of God' is to say what it is not. This
'Love' - for the word *love* has unfortunately many meanings -
has no opposite when referred to God's Love. For, as the hymn
says: 'in God there is no East or West". This means that God's
attributes, including Beauty and Truth, have no opposite. God's
Love is not the love we can have for a greatly desired thing; the
possession of which once gained becomes ultimately a loss or
an irrelevance. God's Love is not the 'Eros' love that a person can
have for another and which in time has the possibility of turning
into its opposite, which is hate or suffering. Again God's Love is
not the love of knowledge, or indeed of truth or of ideals. It was
the mistake of those who would put the intellectual pursuit of
truth before the acceptance of God's Love that Jesus confronted

when he retorted: 'I do not accept praise from men, but I know you. I know that you do not have God's love in your hearts.'[103] Paul's great hymn to Love expresses much of what Love is not, as well as listing some of its properties[104] It is God's Love which precedes our love of God; for He loved us while we were yet unloving sinners.[105]

God's Love is here and now: for God is Love.[106]   So how do we know that God does actually Love us? We can believe intellectually that it is true, that God is Love. As Christians we believe God's Love was shown by His sending Jesus to be our Saviour. But how can we *know* God's Love; not through belief in what we have been told by someone else, but as a fact? When we believe something strongly enough that belief becomes our reality; but is it necessarily true? Will we ever know the Love of God through getting more information, reading more books, listening to more teaching from X, Y or Z?

What are the problems that are in the way? Could it be that one feels that it is impossible, or that one is unworthy, to experience the actuality of God's loving presence? On wishing for a kiss from a loved one would we not be far happier to experience their kiss, rather than being given a written 'X' on a piece of paper?[107] The spoken words of love to God or the sung worship expressing our love - together with the feelings of devotion which this can engender - can be necessary and good. But is this as far as we can go? Can it be only through abstract thought and words that we love God? Is it possible to experience God as closely as one experiences the closeness of a person one loves - even closer? Can we, as it were, go deeper and experience God Himself? We are not, of course, referring to the face-to-face 'Beatific Vision' of God, which has been the experience claimed by some in the past. Again the questions are not '*How* are we to know God's Love? What must we do?' For, in the same way as the receiving of the grace of God, we can do nothing *positively* of ourselves.

All one can do is remove the barriers. All that can be done is to, as mentioned before, open the window and then wait for the breeze to enter the room[108]

For those who neither feel the warmth of God's Love nor experience the Light of God's Love the question is: *Why* do we not experience God's Love?'

The problems of preparing for the coming of Jesus seem to be similar to those of our being aware of God coming into our lives. John the Baptist tried to get the people ready for the coming of Jesus by commanding: 'Prepare the way of the Lord, make straight paths for him' and that 'Every valley shall be filled in and every mountain and hill levelled off'[109] Through what medium is the Lord's path? Is there any other medium than through our consciousness? Is this not a problem concerned with the mind? Have not our minds to 'be still' in order to 'know'?[110] Our minds need to move, that is to think, in order to communicate - just as we are doing now in the writing and the reading of this article. But is it not our thoughts, ideas, ideals, imagination that could be the things which hinder, or 'make hilly', the realisation of the actuality of God? We discover, if we try, that it is very difficult to slow down and control our thoughts. If we do try we only strengthen them. The sense of 'me' would disappear without the continuous stream of thoughts running through our minds - and the sense of 'me' wishes to survive at all costs! It seems that all we can do is be aware, without making any choice, of our mind and its activity - that is without judgement or criticism. 'Judge not' [111] can refer to self-judgement, in particular to our mind-activity. This is because it is the mind itself that is doing the judging - ever circulating and strengthening itself. To think that this will lead to uncontrolled license is to misunderstand the difference between the *self-control* which needs so much effort with so little reward, and the self-control gained by the *control of self*, which requires 'simply' watching.

It is *watching* which produces self-knowledge. Thinking this 'lack of effort to control one's self' will produce uncontrolled behaviour leading to anarchy is similar to the misunderstanding by those who think that they can go on sinning simply because their sins are forgiven anyway, through Christ[112] This control of self, through awareness of the way our mind works, leads to the self-control that Peter refers to.[113] Jesus used the word in this way in the parable of the Ten Young Women[114] 'keep watch'.

Can *keeping this watch* reduce the mind's activities. This activity must create a barrier, or veil, which prevents the experiencing of that 'new life' which is a life lived in the light of God's Love. Our mind activity can so easily creep in 'like a thief in the night' preventing a person from being awake to 'the Master's return.' [115]

Whatever we are doing, reading this for example, is it possible to be aware of God's Love - at this moment? Can praying the Grace tear the veil exposing both believer and seeker alike to the ever present, very real but seemingly hidden Love of God? And can it happen *now*, for love exists only at this present moment?

Dame Julian of Norwich spoke of a series of visions that she had experienced over a period of time. They stressed vividly the crucifixion of Jesus. On pondering the meaning of them, she came to know the incredible love that God had for her and her fellow people. She called these visions 'Revelations of Love.'

She came to know after much pondering as to their meaning:

Would you know the meaning of this thing? Know it well:
Love was his meaning.
Who showed it you? Love.
What showed Him you? Love.

Why did He show it? for Love ....
Thus, I learned that Love is our Lord's meaning.

> > > > >

THE GRACE - 3

Some Thoughts (3)

> The Grace of our Lord Jesus Christ, And the Love of God,
> And the **Fellowship of the Holy Spirit**,
> Be with us all, ever more.

 In the prayer we call 'The Grace' we pray that *'the Fellowship of the Holy Spirit'* be with us all. How would you explain what is behind this to a typical seeker of today? With the provisos made in the first part, here are some personal thoughts and questions on this third part of the prayer.

The meaning of *fellowship* is understandable because we all can experience it for ourselves. Picking out the seemingly relevant meaning from the dictionary, it says: a *fellow* is one who is a companion and equal; and that *fellowship* is the state of being a fellow, a partner, friendly intercourse or communion.
If we look at God with the only feeling that "I am too sinful to get near to Him; He is too holy, He is far transcendent - above me" we can find it hard to believe that we can have the above kind of fellowship with God. This aspect stems from the Old Testament. But through the teaching and life of Jesus we came to learn more fully that there was a different aspect of God. Jesus taught that God was also immanent - close to us; calling Him 'Father, Abba'[116] The Christian claims every Sunday in the Creed that: 'He came down from heaven; ... he became incarnate of the Virgin Mary and was made a person' - just like us. A name given to Jesus was: 'Immanuel' meaning: 'God with us'[117] On Jesus'

death God did not leave us, as it were, bereft.[118] Just as God was in Jesus, so God is the Holy Spirit, Who is in us. As promised we do have the fellowship of the Holy Spirit-[119] In the list of the Holy Spirit's fruit is love, joy and peace.[120] In praying for the fellowship of the Holy Spirit for each other we are praying that this fruit be realised in each of our lives.

Are we actually in fellowship or union with God, the Holy Spirit? Can we generally, experience God closely in our life - just as close, if not closer, than we experience the closeness of the person we love near us? In other words can we have fellowship, or union, with God in our everyday life? Union with the one loved is the ultimate desire of a lover. Paul writes that: 'In Him we move and have our dwelling.'[121] He is nearer to us than our very selves. Mentioning our 'selves' may give a clue to the problem. Do our minds make us think that God is remote? My 'me', thinking itself as being the centre, creates my 'I' as the subject; thus making God similar to an object.

Before his death Jesus spelled it out clearly: ' .. you will *realise* that I am in the Father, and you are in me, and I am in you.'[122] The logic seems clear - even if we cannot think in terms of volume or any other physical property: if A is in B and B is in A then the two are one. The Christian conclusion is that Jesus was perfect man and perfect God. And, perhaps we can ask the question, who are we - actually?

Because God is Who He is, is it a surprise that each of these three sections of the Grace all refer to and include each other? The Grace obviously refers to the Christian tenet, the Trinity of God, which describes God as Father, Son and Holy Spirit. This means that 'Three is One' and 'One is Three'. So we accept that there is Diversity in Unity and Unity in Diversity. Can we not also accept the paradoxical fact that although we are individual, diverse people we are also really in unity one with another? This can be expressed by saying that we all 'share' the One Holy Spirit, Who is obviously not divisible. It is said in the Communion service:

'Though we are many we are one body .....'.

This can mean: we are indeed individuals, but separated only on the physical outside. At a deeper level we are 'spiritually' at one, or united, with each other. Because of this unity with each other there can be fellowship. We can also see that each one of us is a microcosm of everyone else. Physically we have all inherited the same instincts of evolution, we all experience the same feelings of fear, joy, love, suffering, anxiety; we all share the same environment; we all share with each other through our senses and our compassion, we all depend on each other. It is not my world, it is not your world, it is *our* world, just as God is *our* Father. When we pray for God's Grace, Love and Fellowship 'be with us all', who are the 'we' that we are praying for? Jesus commanded us to love one another.[123] Is it possible for Christians and unknowingly for them, non-Christians to see that the Holy Spirit is within *everyone*, as John proclaimed[124] ... and so honour him or her accordingly. There is a tradition for some in the East that when people meet, they put their hands together and bow to one another, respecting Who they are meeting. So would it not be a fantastic leap forward for peace in the world if we identified ourselves, not as separate individuals defending our own little corners, but as humans, part of one body, humanity? Paul states that, in God's eyes, there is no distinction between race, social class or gender.[125] Are not our mind-driven groupings, of nationalism, for instance, in which we wrap ourselves in our flags, alien to God who we pray to in the Grace? We join groups for, we think, security. But it is this very splitting of humanity into false, mind-produced groupings which has led to this very insecurity. It has inevitably resulted in wars since the beginning of time (an estimated 100 million killed by war in the last century alone). So what is the answer to the problem of man's inhumanity to man? Surely it is Love. This sounds rather naive in today's world of competition, selfishness, identification, and pre-emptive strikes.

However, there is Someone who gave this answer to our present disastrous predicament two thousand years ago! He went so far as to command us to love even our enemies.[126]

*****

The series concluded with this afterword:

These three articles are by their nature *thoughts*, in the form of *opinions*; and therefore these are by their very nature *'dual'*. That is: for every thought there will be its 'reverse', or opposite. For example: any political, economic or religious opinion will have an opposite view. As an example, coincidently, X's article in the May issue gives an interesting example of the fragmentation which thought causes. He described just *one* part of the Church of England as having *three* strands of belief. The strands he named *'Canal'*, *'River'* and *'Charismatic.'* The first is composed of people who are Conservative and believe in the inerrancy of Scripture. The second are people who are Open and believe in the intrinsic authority of Scripture. Lastly, the third strand is made up of those who believe in the authority and trustworthiness of Scripture.

So, these articles I know will not be exempt from opposing opinions! However, one opinion which I hope we can all share is that we can give thanks at all times for the boundless gifts of God's Grace, Love and Fellowship. We would hope also that our open-minded enquirer would not only hear but also see the fruits of this in the Church and be encouraged at the least to make further enquiry.

****

APPENDIX C – THE POSITIVE APPROACH

It was stated, at the end of Chapter 7, that our knowledge comes from two inborn mental powers. One may be named 'scientific' as it gives us knowledge of things on the *outside*—on the physical plane and processed by reason. The other may be named 'mystic,' or 'spiritual / religious;' as it enlightens us from a deeper—*inside*—level using insight or intuition.

The branch of philosophy, called 'metaphysics,' which deals with the first principles of things - including abstract concepts such as being, knowing, identity, time, and space - is an attempt to consider the world as a whole, by means of thought. So, one can see it is firmly in the A-mode. It has been developed, from the beginning, by the union and conflict of these two different human drives: the scientific and the mystical or spiritual.

Some people are attracted to scientific knowledge. This has led many to picture a purely material world. Using true intellectual honestly, these, by their basing their search for Reality on science, can find it difficult to see any place in the universe for 'God,' or even, for some, Love.

As a metaphor, when watching a film using a DVD, they search for the reality of its film, say, by discovering that it is a product of digital signals. These being in the form of 0's and 1's, by the use of lasers and the lighting up of pixels on a screen, and so on. They search for Reality on the 'outside.'

Other people, recognising that there have been many discarded images of 'God' over the past – such as God having human form or attributes - have discovered new ways of *seeing* God with new eyes. They discover a God that is not dead. Understanding that 'God is Spirit' (John 4:24) opens one to the belief that God is not limited – to either 'outer' or 'inner.' Spirit is everywhere and, like the wind (John 3:8), one does not know from where IT comes, or to where IT goes. Similarly, the unseen Spirit can only be known by its effects. So today, many with equal intellectual honestly, are open to the possibility that there is a place for 'God.' These are people who are attracted towards mystical, or spiritual knowledge. As the study developed, it was this experiential 'inner' path that was taken eventually. Repeating the use of the above metaphor, when watching the film using a DVD, they search for Reality on the 'inside,' by discovering the *story* of the film.

#

In order to inquire into Reality or Truth, the study used simple and straight forward definitions: *reality* is what is real to us; *actuality* is what is actual, factual, or given in our experience. For instance, for a 'flat earth' believer, a flat earth will be his *reality* - he will see it as flat - but his reality will not be the *actuality*.

Both the science and the mystic paths have had their great champions; those who base their quest for Reality through the senses and those who use their insight to tell the story. But the greatest philosophers have been those who have felt the need for both scientific facts and mystic insights. These philosophers, ancient and modern, by attempting to harmonise the two, have made philosophy greater than either alone.

In this appendix C, these two positive philosophic approaches will be very briefly considered.

#

The main study came to the point that only through walking the mystical/spiritual path – in the P-mode - would one ultimately come across 'Truth.' But there was a proviso that the insightful findings were subjected to 'scientific' consideration.

 So, both paths are necessary and, of course, both have their dangers.

#

Questions are raised, such as: What is Truth? and What is mind/brain relationship? What is consciousness – the modes of which are so important?

What have the two streams of philosophy to say?

#

One's answer to the question: 'Which of the two streams of philosophy should one choose to view the Reality which forms our basic attitude to life?' is largely influenced by one's view point.

Beginning early in life, we gradually form a set of beliefs and ideas which tell us what our relationship is to ourselves and the world; what our world view is: our Reality. We form answers, even if they are not consciously put into words. These affect our minds and actions, and the way we answer questions such as 'Who am I, as an individual?' and 'What is my role in society?' So, our worldview is very important.

It is difficult to develop an independent personal world view which is unbiased. One is surrounded by pressures from one's parents, friends, educational establishments, the media, with its much inane content and advertisements, twenty-four-hour news programs, political opinions and so on. But now, to increase the pressure even more, thrown into the mix is the internet with its social media.

Each of us in society forms our specific personal viewpoint. There is no common, agreed worldview at this level of society. In society, groups are formed which have specific agendas, together with the groups who naturally have opposite agendas. All these factions exist together in our society. They range across environmentalists, conservationists, developers, religious fundamentalists, agnostics, vegans, materialists, political and social activists, and so on. All, being in the A-mode, will have their opposing groups.

Chapter 4, Our Homemade World, drew attention to the fact, that thought influences this system of ideas and beliefs held throughout society.

However, the majority of society, beneath each specific personal viewpoint, accepts, possibly tacitly, a set of ideas and beliefs that are assumed throughout society: society's viewpoint. This set forms the world views which are held by society in general. For many years in the Western World, science has been the most influential factor in forming these philosophical ideas and beliefs.

The following are two brief examples of the main philosophical approaches: the scientific and the mystical.

#

1 - SCIENCE

For the last three hundred years science has had the most influence on Western society. Before then, religion was the dominant influence. Science has grown to be the background to society's main core worldview. The science-based philosophy, named Materialism, came about during, what is called, the 'Age of Enlightenment.' It began around the late 17 and early 18th centuries, when it became the foundation of modern western political and intellectual culture. The pioneers believed that human logic, or science and mathematics, would overcome the prevailing suffering brought about by superstition, religion and conflict. Thus, they thought a better world would be brought about. The Enlightenment gave special importance to reason, and the evidence of the senses as the primary sources of knowledge, rather than tradition – such as given beliefs. In other words, science became the trusted defender of Truth, having driven religion from that position. From this, it can be seen that to many scientists, even today, any thought of bringing non-material phenomena, such as consciousness and mind, into any scientific enquiry, in order to help explain Reality, is anathema and must not be entertained.

#

Metaphysical Materialism is the idea that there is nothing in our experience that cannot be explained by the physical brain and its processes within it.

Materialism claims that reality exists outside of your mind in the form of material reality. So, reality exists outside your mind in the form of material particles. But then, if *only* material things are real, it is believed that all things such as mind, consciousness and thoughts will be explained, eventually, by the way material things interact. So, according to Materialism - although these brain processes are electro-chemical in nature - mind, consciousness and thoughts, are the results of chance arrangements of particles of matter produced in the processes of the brain. An article in the 2021 October issue of The Radio Times, reports Brian Cox, who is the Royal Society's 'Professor for public engagement in science,' saying: "We're no more than a collection of atoms that can think."

Here we have in more detail the brain/mind problem, which was met with briefly in the study. There it was said: 'therefore, whatever the scientific explanations of mind/brain relationship are, it is taken experientially that the mind is intimately related to and has a great influence on the brain.'

At the beginning of the 20c, scientific discoveries - which produced the revolutionary science of Quantum Mechanics - disputed the metaphysical assumptions underlying scientific materialism. It showed that atoms and their sub-atomic particles are not objects, but show tendencies to exist and that there was dependence on the observer, amongst many other surprising discoveries.

Today there is a growing number of scientists who realise that they need to take account of human experience; the inner as well as the outer phenomena. They are open to taking into account the field of consciousness and mind. This requires the interpretation of natural phenomena; a change from analysis to synthesis. The scientific results, of this now emerging 'Third Scientific Revolution,' has thrown over the old Materialistic metaphysic which has dominated science over the last few hundred years.

The future promise is that science will produce, for instance, explanations for the unexpected, ever-developing complexity of life. In time no doubt, science will make continued progress towards discovering the mysterious forces which have produced our self-awareness, our feeling and consciousness of life, and the mystery of 'I Am.'

Maybe we will get answers to such a question as:
'Is perhaps the fact being:
　　　　The brain is in the Mind, rather than the
　　　　　　mind being in the brain?

#

This study avoided discussing theories concerning these mysteries—whether scientific, philosophical or theological — except to refer to them briefly, where it was helpful. The study's approach was to look at mankind's mysteries through our own individual *experiences; that is to follow the mystical path; but also referring to the scientific to round off any insights raised.*
In other words, for everyday life, now, referring to the specific question mentioned above - 'What is Reality?' – we make use of our own experience of *reality* and *consciousness*.

So, in the West we have looked at science to tell us what the facts are. It is in the West, for hundreds of years, that we have looked to science to tell us what truth is; and it has been science which we trust to give us the correct answers. But as mentioned above, a philosophy which includes both science and mysticism is probably the wisest path.

>>>>

2 - MYSTICISM

In the second part of this appendix, we will look at the thoughts of just one particular Christian theologian, as an example of a positive mystical, religious approach.

◆ ◆ ◆

Main stream Christianity believes that there is one God; as does Judaism and Islam.

But there is here a practical difference between a 'religion' and 'mystical spirituality'. Simply put, in this study the difference between the two:

a 'religious' person believes that the one God is monistic: God having absolute power. Such a person has a world view focused on science's *objective* understanding of the world.

a 'mystic,' person has a world view which is focused on the mystical, *subjective* understanding of the world. However, a mystical theologian will usually be affiliated to a particular religion and a specific branch of that religion.

This is no place to try to understand the many theological explanations, arguments and counter-arguments which will be produced by almost every philosophical or theological topic in the A-mode.

#

Referring to a quote at the study's outset, here I am metaphorically *'collecting flowers,'* from the theologian, Raimon Panikkar.

He is chosen as being among those 'open' to constructive criticism regarding the Christian religion. The topic chosen is the dogma regarding 'God.' The following are some of his thoughts – at least my understanding of them. Needless to say, reading his actual writings is the only satisfactory way to the proper understanding of his thoughts.

A Christian theologian has been chosen due to the writer's limited experience of other religions. Other religions, beliefs and so on, can repeat the exercise; provided they are ones that can point towards the truth.

#

Years before interfaith studies became all the rage, he, a Catholic priest, asserted that the Western Christian Church could learn from Eastern religions. In the 1970's he was teaching at the University of California. This was the period during which was established Suzuki's Zen centre, that was spreading its influence throughout the world. Not surprisingly in such a flourishing centre, there were also three of my early influential writers: the Christian ex-priest Alan Watts (whose books on the Christian and Eastern religions, first claimed my attention), and Aldous Huxley (whose *Perennial Philosophy* was eye-opening).   Also, at the time, Jiddu Krishnamurti (who sparked my wish to understand more) owned property at Ojai nearby the University.

#

The central dogma of Christianity is that God is the 'Trinity.' Panikkar states the need for Christians to rediscover the Christian *Trinitarian* God. Many Christians themselves barely know of its underlying meaning. As a result, it has little or no effect on their lives.

#

The early followers of Jesus had the problem of coming to an understanding of the nature of God. They needed answers as to the nature of Jesus in relation to God, and what the implications were. In the Gospels, Jesus presented himself as divine image when, at the same time, being a fully human being. He referred to Himself as God's Son; to have God as his Father (John 10:36,37). He said 'I and the Father are one' (Jn10:30). In saying this, he was claiming, whilst being fully human, to be one with God. Inevitably he was accused of blasphemy: 'Because you, being a man, make yourself God' (John 10:33.)

#

In the first centuries after the death of Jesus, the doctrine of the Trinity grew and matured by reflection on the faith. Although the word 'Trinity' does not appear in the scriptures, it was seen that the Incarnation made no sense without the concept of a Trinitarian God.

#

So, the Trinity was formed, not only from the fact that Jesus was fully human, but also that He claimed: 'The Father and I are one' (John 10:30). This is a statement about the relationship between Father and Son. As there are these two factors – a *communion* and a *distinction* - within the one statement, it can only be taken as a condition of non-duality*. There is:
(1) an internal *communion* (between the 'Father and I'), which makes them inseparable: *they are one.*
(2) a *distinction* between them (between the 'Father and I'). They are inseparable yet distinct, at the same time.
Here, the dualistic term 'non-duality' is taken to represent the condition in which explicit differences have implicit unity.

After his resurrection, Jesus the historical man, becomes The Christ: Christ Jesus, the second 'Person' of the Trinity. (It may be pointed out here, that this term 'Persons' has nothing to do withSelfness of Personality discussed in Chapter 5.)Jesus Christ, who was before his death a historical man, said that He must leave His disciples so that the Spirit (the third 'Person') could come to be with them. Thus, when referring to either of the three 'Persons', the other two are inferred. The reference is to God: The Unbroken Trinity.

The main insight of Trinity is clearly *relationship*. The Trinity is dynamic; it is in constant movement. It is said that the Son is *begotten* of the Father, and, the Holy Spirit *proceeds* from the Father and through the Son. The Father never ceases to beget the Son, nor the Son to be begotten.[127] The Spirit is the permanent expression of their dynamism. There is relationship between the Three. There can be no hierarchy between the 'Persons.'

Though not distinct from them, the *Godhead* underlies the three Persons. There are three relationships in the non-dual being of the Godhead: The eternal Father as the subject, the eternal Son as the object and the eternal Holy Spirit as the verb. That is: the lover, the beloved and the love.

#

The difficulty for the early Christians was to preach a message; a message which, at that time, was so unfamiliar to that of the then existing Hellenistic-Jewish culture and language.

During these years, in the early church there was much controversy. One such controversy being the scriptures themselves. Some followers wished to dissociate the New from the Old Testament. The God of the Hebrews, they said, cannot be the Father of our Lord Jesus Christ. More recently, it has been said that:

'On the whole, the uncritical acceptance of the Jewish scriptures has been a very doubtful boon to the church,'

(W.R. Inge, Dean of St Paul's 1911 to 1934).

#

However, Christianity became the state religion after

Constantine's adopted it for his empire, and thus it became political. A monistic belief, a belief in one God, suited a reigning tyrant. The imperial policy thus embraced monotheism. The Trinity is a challenge to any kind of imperialism. So over time the trinitarian scandal, that cost Jesus his life, became blurred.

#

Pannikar sees the Christian message differing, unfortunately, quite significantly from Judaism. Sadly, this has led to unnecessary conflicts between the two religions. The traditional early Christian Trinity doctrine was entangled fundamentally with the interweaving of two traditions: the Semitic and the Greek. As quoted at the end of the study, Paul said that the riddle of the Christian message – the Crucifixion - is a stumbling block to the minds of the Jews, and is foolishness to the logical Greeks. [1 Cor 1:23]

The Jewish traditional importance of history has restricted the Christian God to being the 'Lord of History.' But, although Christianity, as a religion, is a religion having a historical basic story, Christianity itself is timeless. This is due to the fact that Jesus, a historical man, became the ascended Christ, who lives in the present, now. The Christian Trinitarian God is not tied to the past. Christians worship the Trinitarian God, in whom time is the eternal *Now*. For the Christian, the experience of Jesus is the present experience of the risen Christ Jesus (together, of course, with the unbroken Trinity, of Father and Holy Spirit: God). This experience is not historical, it occurs now and cannot be passed on second-hand – it cannot be told.

One final comment on Panikkar's theology, he forecasts that the Christian of tomorrow will either be mystical or she will not even exist. Christianity, he says, should be transformed with the indispensable help of mysticism. The present spiritual leadership is failing to instil a consciousness of the 'Beyond' at the deeper, mystical level.

#

The reason I used Christianity, as an example for the Positive approach to truth, was given above. It is stressed that any religion or philosophy can be used as an example, provided it is based on mysticism. Throughout, there has been no purposely-made criticism of any religious belief, or no belief.

Only when the conceptual framework, which we have superimposed over 'That Which Is', is demolished - that is when the Self is no longer identified with the ego-self and stripped of all concepts - then it simply knows that it is eternal and whole. On realisation, this knowing is so certain that any doubt seems impossible. We cannot use words to convince anyone of this experience; it cannot be told.

#

So, reference here is made back to Nicholas de Cusa's metaphor. This concerned the door, in the surrounding wall of the Divine Garden. From the beginning of history, people have passed by the door. Some taking no notice of it. Some have glimpsed, beyond the partly opened door, into the Garden; wondering what life would be like beyond the wall. Now and then, someone walks through the door. The Garden, it seems, can be given many names; by the Muslim, Jannah; by the Buddhist, Nirvana, Liberation; by the Christian, Heaven; by the Hindu, Moksha; by the Daoist, the axis, the empty centre of the hub; and so on and on. But in the Garden, there are no names. We know, however, that the meaning can only be one.

#

It seems that the realisation of 'God' – however realised, whatever your insight as to the divine, whatever your traditional viewpoint - is necessary to human wellbeing and without which society will continue to circle down into continued chaos.

The prayer is that in Love all may be One.

#

A final reminder: that whatever A-mode opinion is stated in this Appendix C, the study claims that *Truth cannot be Told.*

****

Grace and Peace be with you.

****

---

[1]Lord Winston, an eminent scientist, also admitted that he was religious, but would not then go into what he meant by this. BBC, Radio 4, June 2005.

[2]Ref.: Mat 12:45; Lk 11:26. The casting out of one undesirable allowed many more to eventually enter.

[3]This could be named as 'Law of Unintended Consequences' or 'Law of Reverse Effect'.

[4]John 9:39. By the way, this is another example of reverse effect.

[5]John 14:4-6

[6] Quoting his words, Jesus' positive approach must not be taken anywhere in this study to be anything other than what he is reported to have said. This is obeying the rules stated above. This passage is used as an example of the Positive Approach.

[7] It was mentioned in Chapter 2: 'Often we approach these (three) mysteries of life in a piecemeal fashion: one at a time .....and it is not suggested that we should.'

[8]Jesus said that force cannot be used:
From the days of John the Baptist until now the kingdom of Heaven has been the subject of force and violent men are trying to seize it.

[9]When in this exercise we refer to 'a need' to do something, this is not to be taken as a method!

[10]Here is also an example that the answer to a problem is in the problem itself.

[11] Intrinsic: Belonging naturally, inherent, essential (Oxford Dictionary)

[12] For instance, how many attempts are there to explain why God wipes out the entire human population and animal kingdom, except for those in the Ark, because people did not obey Him?

[13]There is usually *ltlite dciflfutiy in udrendsnatnig*, even when the letters are in the wrong order, provided the first and last letters are correct.

[14]Realise: To bring home to one's experience (Chambers Dictionary).

[15]The three taken from The Oxford Dictionary of Quotations

[16]Galations: 3:28. Not unaturally, he uses this in the Christian context, for he says:'...for you are all one in Christ.' This need not be limited solely to Christianity.

Refer also to Colossians 3:11

[17]Richard Dawkins' referred to the belief that *outward* evidence for the evolutionary theory, introduced by Darwin, is now supported by the new *inward* evidence which has been produced recently by gene research. A rat shares many similar genes to the mouse; as do humans and apes. We should be proud, he says, of the fact that *every* ancestor of ours has survived to maturity and has produced offspring. Every living creature has inherited successful genes from an unbroken line, whatever the vicissitudes of their lives. He maintains that this gene research shows that through DNA: 'The tree of *all* life relates to *every* living being on this planet.' (Television series, part 3, 2008.) This view is, of course, disputed by Creationists. (Again, there is no judgment being intended in this study on this or any other opinion or belief.)

[18] With regret one has to write: 'to this day'— This study was partly motivated by this problem, as mentioned in the Introduction.

One has sympathy with Chuang Tzu (370-287 BCE) when he said:

"Great truths do not take hold of the hearts of the masses. And now, as the world is in error, how shall I, though I know the true path, how shall I guide? If I know that I cannot succeed and yet try to force success, this would be but another source of error. Better then to desist and strive no more. But if I do not strive, who will?"

[19] Another example of the mind trying to correct a problem which was produced by the mind itself.

[20] The question of the mind/brain relationship can only, in this study, be briefly touched on. How **'That Which Is'** is experienced is of paramount interest from the study's point of view. We have a brain and we experience a mind which operates in it. The importance of theories concerning the mind/brain is not ignored, but they have to be left for discussion elsewhere.

[21] Romeo and Juliet

[22] The question 'How can this be achieved?' will be discussed in a later chapter.

[23]'Chronological time' is time measured by the clock. It can be contrasted to another type of time, *psychological* time. This other kind of time stems from the mind and will be considered further later.

[24]Example suggested by John Humphries 'Lost for Words', Hodder and Stoughton, 2004.

[25]*Thinking, Fast and Slow* by D. Kahneman.

[26] A system is a set of connected things or parts which are mutually dependent. This dependence being on their meaning and existence as well as their mutual action.

[27] REFLEX is produced by or concerned with response from a nerve-centre to a stimulus from outside; it is an involuntary response.

[28] Referring to the story in Genesis Chapter 32

[29] King Midas found that you cannot eat money.

[30]Percept: (philosophical use) Object of perception; mental product as opposed to the action of perceiving.

[31] Note that we are, as is usual in this study, referring to *psychological* problems.   Everyday factual problems do have the possibility of being satisfactorily sorted out, of course, through thoughtful reasoning.

[32] John 12:24

[33] *As You Like It.* Act 2

[34] *The Tempest.* Act 4

[35] John 8:58

[36]Matthew 16:15. 'But what about you? Who do you say I am?'

[37] It can be thought by some to have been dealt with fairly unsatisfactorily. His will be considered more fully in Appendix C.

[38] To many believing Christian every word of the New Testament is to be accepted. However this is not in the remit of this study. These matters must be left to the theologians. Here it is of interest—by noting some of what he is reported to have done and said—to see into the mind of such an influential person as Jesus. The study does not set out to prove or disprove what actually happened in the past. The study's concern is with *now*.

[39] This extract from Paul was chosen as an example, in a religious context, of the concept of a 'veil' hiding the truth. There is no implication that it be taken as being 'true'. Such 'positive' statements are not allowed to be made in the study.

[40] Mind, being intimately related to brain, will be referred to as' brain/mind' where appropriate.

[41] Here we are beginning tentatively to take the dualist view of mind as more reasonable, but no less mysterious!

[42]The well-known proverb *"Know Thyself"* was carved over the door to the Temple at Delphi.

[43] At this point we can assume that there may be other 'levels' of consciousness besides that referred to above.

[44]In religious terms: We would know that we were all embraced in one-ness by the All-knowing, All-Loving God/Creator/Being.

[45] About which more needs to be said later in the study.

[46]Matt 11:28

[47] It is worth asking the question: Who or what is doing the driving?! It is, of course, the mind.

[48] These are positive statements and care must therefore be exercised as to

their pointing to the truth.

[49] Referred to again below.

[50] Mark 2:27

[51]*Persona*: The outermost part of the consciousness, the expression of the personality. Roman actor's mask [Latin. A player's mask, perhaps from Etruscan: masked figures] (Chambers Dictionary)

[52]*Person*: Character represented, as on a stage; a capacity in which one is acting; a self-conscious being; a personality etc.. (Chambers Dictionary)

[53] In Chapter 3, Jesus was quoted as saying that force cannot be used to enter the kingdom. The 'kingdom' is not a thing that can be attained or achieved by one's own efforts—'but by grace alone'.

[54] Insight and realisation will be the subject of a later chapter.

[55]Matt 16:23. Of course a Christian believes that only Jesus can make demands like this.

[56] Reality; that is what seems real to us.

[57] A - standing for Analogy

[58]Analogy: an agreement or relationship in certain respects between things which are otherwise different.

[59] This world is what Jesus referred to when he said: "I have told you these things, so that in me you may have peace. In this world you will have trouble. But take heart! I have overcome the world." [John 16:33]

[60]Of course, because all of this *is* in the A-mode, it *is certain* that there will be controversy over the examples chosen! This study itself, keeping to its Approach, is not implying that any of these statements are 'true' or not, or are appropriate or not! But this attempt to avoid using opinions—they being only the writer's suggestions—leaves the individual to come across the truth him or herself. To repeat: nobody else can do it for someone else. This keeps to the Approach adopted for this study.

[61] Succession: A coming after or a following: a sequence in time and place: law, recognised mode, right, order or turn, of succeeding one to another.
(*Chambers 20th c Dictionary*)

[62] Referred to in Hardy's poems, Chapter 1.

[63] At the end of the study, it having been completed and its rules being no longer applicable, an After Note, containing some (positive) comments, will be made.

[64] To be considered further in the next chapter

[65] A reminder that this discussion refers to our *psychological* P-mode status and not our everyday A-mode. This may not seem practical; but psychologically, therefore practically, it is immensely so.

[66] '**Here I am!** I stand at the door and knock. If anyone hears my voice and

opens the door, I will come in and eat with him and he with me.'

In other words, in Christian terms, Christ Jesus enters our consciousness and there is a relationship with the Spirit. Ref: Revelations 3:20

[67] This light is said to have been brought into our world by Jesus. Hence his being described as 'the light of the world.'

[68] Notice the negatives: the negative approach is used in order to enter the P-mode. This is an example of a negative approach producing positive results.

[69] This is now looking at the third mystery of Chapter 2: The Beyond, referring to That Which Is *beyond* our rational thought.

[70] The Tao is a fundamental idea in most Chinese philosophic schools. It denotes the Truth or proposition that is the origin, basis and foundation of everything that exists.

[71]Eph 2:8. This may seem to be equating the Holy Spirit with this 'intelligence'. This is left to the reader to decide; as positive suggestions are not actually allowed in the rules of the study.

[72]*Metaphysics*: The science which investigates the first principles of nature and thought; ontology* or the science of being. N*ote that here it does not refer to other applications such as:* supernatural, fanciful or 'addicted to far-fetched conceits'! - *Chambers Dictionary.*

*Ontology is a system of belief that reflects an interpretation by an individual about what constitutes a fact.

[73] Ephesians 2:6

[74] John 14:20

[75] Luke 18:26,27

[76] Psyche: we have a body, which is always in time; a spirit which is always timeless; and psyche which is associated with the body to some extent but capable of being identified with the spirit, and through its spirit with the divine Ground.

[77] 1Cor 3:16; 6:19 and 2Cor 6:16·

[78] Ref: Revelations 3:20

[79] John 1:9

[80] Matt 8:22

[81] 1Peter 2:9

[82] Remembering that these can and should be tested.

[83] Examples of THIS and THAT.

(1) Using Negative approach (*Chuang Tzu, Chinese c330-275BCE*): 'Where all opposites meet, the distinction between 'this' and 'that' does not really exist. When both 'this', which is subjective, and 'that,' which is objective, are correlated, then this is the very centre – or Axis - at which all Infinities converge; they combine into the infinite One.'

(2) Using Positive approach (*Eckhart, German c1260-1327*): 'As long as I am this or that, or have this or that, I am not all things and I have not all things. Become pure till you are neither nor have this or that; then you are omnipresent and being neither this nor that are all things.'

[84] Referring to two books by W. Inge (1860-1954), the earlier book on mysticism (1899) refers to Eastern religions describing them as *nihilistic*. By the second book listed (1948), which was his last, he was acknowledging his interest in Eastern thought; what he termed 'Indian' thinking.

[85] John 1:17

[86] I Peter 3: 15. 'Always be prepared to give an answer to everyone who asks you to give the reason for the hope that you have. But do this with gentleness and respect ....'

[87] John 1: 14. 'The Word became flesh and made his dwelling among us. We have seen his glory, the glory of the One and Only, who came from the Father, full of grace and truth.'

[88] Luke 2:40

[89] John 1: 16,17

[90] 1 Cor 1: 3; 2 Cor 1: 2; Gall: 3; Phil 1: 2 and so on.

[91] Rom 16:20,24; l Car 16:23 and so on.

[92] 1 Cor 15:10

[93] John 14:9

[94] Eph 2:8,9 'For it is by grace you have been saved, through faith - and this not from yourselves, it is the gift of God - not by works so that no-one can boast.'

[95] Matt 16:24; Mark 8:34; Luke 9:23, 17:33; John 12:25. 'If anyone would come after me, he must deny himself and take up his cross and follow me.' 'If anyone would come after me, he must deny himself and take up his cross daily and follow me.' 'Whoever tries to keep his life will lose it, and whoever will lose his life will keep it.' 'The man who loves his life will lose it, while the man who hates his life in this world will keep it for eternal life. Whoever serves me will follow me; and where I am my servant will also be.'

[96] For example, Luke 12:25. 'Who of you by worrying can add a single hour to his life?'

[97] For example, Matt 7: 1, 'Do not judge, or you too will be judged.'

[98] 2 Cor 12:9. Paul reports: 'He said to me, "My grace is sufficient for you, for my power is made perfect in weakness."'

[99] Matt 28:20. Matthew reports Jesus' last words spoken in his gospel: "And surely I am with you always, to the very end of the age."

[100]Rev 3:20. "Here I am! I stand at the door and knock. If anyone hears my voice and opens the door, I will come in and eat with him and him with me."

[101]l Peter 2:9. " ... that you may declare the praises of him who called you out of darkness into his wonderful light."

[102]Rom 6:4 'We were therefore buried with him through baptism into death in order that ..... we too may live a new life.'

18 Eph 4:14

[103]John 6: 41,42

[104]l Cor 13.

[105]Rom 5:8 : 'But God demonstrates his own love for us in this: While we were still sinners, Christ died for us.'

[106]IJohn 4:8, 16

[107]Rom I6: 16; 'Greet on another with a holy kiss.'

1 Peter 5: 15. 'Greet one another with a kiss of love.'

[108]John 3:6-8. 'Flesh gives birth to flesh, but the Spirit gives birth to the spirit. You should not be surprised at my saying, "You must be born again." The wind blows wherever it pleases. You hear its sound, but you cannot tell where it comes from or where it is going. So it is with everyone born of the Spirit."

[109]Isaiah 40:3; Matt 3:3; Mark 1:3; Luke 3:4,5; John 1:23.

[110]Ps 46: 10

[111]Matt 7: 1 This judgement can also refer to that of yourself.

[112]Gal 2: 17 'If while I seek to be justified in Christ, it becomes evident that we ourselves are sinners, does that mean that Christ promotes sin? Absolutely not!"

[113] 1 Peter 4:7

[114] Matt 25: 13 'Therefore keep watch ... '

[115] Matt 24:42-44; Mark 13:33, 37 and so on. 'Therefore keep watch because you do not know on what day your Lord will come. .... So you must also be ready ... ' 'Be on your guard, be alert!' 'Therefore keep watch because you do not know when the owner of the house will come back ... What I say to you I say to everyone: Watch!'

[116] Rom 8: 15 'For you did not receive a spirit that makes you a slave again to fear, but you received the Spirit of sonship. And by him we cry "Abba, Father".

[117] Isa 7: 14; Matt 1:23 'The virgin shall be with child and will give birth to a son, and will call him Immanuel'; ' ... and they will call him Immanuel - which means 'God with us.'"

[118] John 14:16,26 ' ... and he will give you another Counsellor to be with you for ever - the Spirit of truth.'

[119] 1 Cor 1:9 'God who has called you into fellowship with his Son Jesus Christ our Lord, is faithful.'

[120] Gal 5:22 'But the fruit of the Spirit is love, joy, peace, patience, kindness, goodness, faithfulness, gentleness and self-control.

[121] Acts 17:28

[122] John 10:30; 14: 10, 11,20

[123] 1 John 4: 19 and so on 'We love one another because he first loved us'.

[124] John 1:4,9 'In him was life, and that life was the light of men. ... The true light that gives light to *every* man was coming into the world.'

[125] Gal 3: 28, Col 3: 11 'There is neither Jew nor Greek, slave nor free, male or female, for you are all one in Christ.'

[126] Matt 5:43,44 'You have heard it was said, 'Love your neighbour and hate your enemy. But I tell you: Love your enemies and pray for those who persecute you.'

[127] This is referred to, in a Christmas Day morning sermon by Meister Eckhart, in which he says: "Here in time, we make holiday because the eternal birth which God the Father bore and bears unceasingly in eternity is now born in time, in human nature." He goes on to stress the individual's responsibility, by asserting this:

"St. Augustine says this birth is always happening. But if it happens not in me, what does it profit me? What matters is that it shall happen in me."

Printed in Great Britain
by Amazon

24350054R00116